Practical Screenwriting

Practical Screenwriting

Charles Deemer

focus Publishing

∾

To my screenwriting students

Past, present and future.

May your stories be filled with a strong sense of

What happens next?

∾

TABLE OF CONTENTS

INTRODUCTION

This book is called *Practical Screenwriting* for a reason. No other form of writing is as collaborative and competitive as screenwriting. Whereas earlier generations of young writers dreamed of penning "the Great American Novel," today they are more likely to aspire to writing a screenplay. At the same time, there is no large readership of screenplays out of the environment of the movie business, most readers being employees of film production companies who read for the most practical of reasons: to decide whether or not to recommend the script at hand for possible production. The only other large group of readers looking at screenplays consists of students trying to learn how to write them. The screenplay, in other words, is rooted firmly in the soil of commerce, and this reality dictates how they are written. It's a practical matter.

Screenplays are written to be read quickly and understood easily. My approach to teaching screenwriting craft begins with this fact.

The ideas I develop in this book evolved during my career as a university and online screenwriting teacher and were first expressed in 1997 in an electronic screenwriting tutorial called *Screenwright: The Craft of Screenwriting*. Along the way, many students and colleagues contributed to what became a unique approach to teaching screenwriting, unique mostly by its admission that there was more than one good way to go about it. *Practical Screenwriting* is, first and foremost, a guide to writing clean, crisp, clear scripts that will get read in the crowded contemporary marketplace. It also represents the culmination of my thinking on the matter as I near retirement.

I am indebted to Ron Pullins of Focus Publishing for encouraging me to adapt my earlier work in screenwriting instruction for a larger audience. Without his initial enthusiasm for such a book, *Practical Screenwriting* would never have been written. Its faults are mine, of course; but its very existence rests on the shoulders of Ron's enthusiasm.

Digital technology already is making changes in the possibilities of film production and distribution. While the new technology also promises new opportunities for screenwriters, what have not changed are the principles of compelling film storytelling.

From the flickering lights of the campfire to the flickering images on a movie screen, the process of narrative magic begins with the storyteller. In film, the storyteller is the screenwriter, and the vehicle for telling a story and beginning the process of filmmaking is the unusual rhetorical document called a screenplay. *Practical Screenwriting* is your guide to mastering its craft.

Charles Deemer
Portland State University
Portland, Oregon

1

Screenwriting:
the Dream v. the Reality

Every year tens of thousands of screenplays are registered with the Writers Guild of America (WGA), the standard industry procedure for protecting one's work.

Every year over 5,000 scripts compete for several Nicholl Screenwriting Fellowships, one of the top prizes for new writers.

The Great American Screenplay

Young writers no longer aspire to write the Great American Novel (as in my generation) but the Great American Screenplay. Not only young writers chase this dream—many older writers have embarked upon a second career, seeking to write the screenplay that will open Hollywood's doors.

Screenwriting may be the most competitive form of writing in today's market. Of the over one hundred thousand scripts written annually, at best only a few hundred become movies. Selling a screenplay is about as likely as winning the lottery (after studying the probabilities, a California mathematics professor concluded you are more likely to win a million playing the lottery!). But there's an essential difference.

A great deal more than luck is involved in writing and selling a screenplay. A little good fortune—being in the right place at the right time with the right script—never hurts. But writing a screenplay is an act of imagination and craft over which you have total control. It is in marketing a screenplay that Lady Luck may come into play. But what you bring to the market is completely up to you. It is here that one writer can gain significant competitive advantage over another.

Earning Good Fortune

Successful screenplays have certain things in common—things that can be learned. Success may not be automatic once you learn the craft of screenwriting, but without learning it, you are at a significant disadvantage.

Producers commonly complain about the number of poorly crafted screenplays entering the market. By mastering the craft of screenwriting, you join an elite group with significantly greater chances of commercial success. The focus of this book is the craft of screenwriting.

The Six Essentials of Screenwriting

There are six essential areas of screenwriting craft:

- **Character Development**: You are telling stories about people. Regardless of how many buildings blow up or how many hostages are taken along the way, your story must have memorable characters. Consider the "characters" in your own life: "Joe or Mary is such a character!" Why do you remember them this way? Because something about them is distinctive. In a larger-than-life medium, it's even more important to create memorable characters.

- **Structure**: "Screenwriting," they say, "is about structure, structure, and structure." Surely no narrative form is more economical or demands more from each word. Much of your time will be devoted to learning structure, or what we call "the 3-act paradigm."

- **Economy**: Two kinds of economy are important in screenwriting: structural economy to ensure efficient scene design, and rhetorical economy that ensures the script is a quick, easy read. A screenplay is not written primarily to be read. The publication of screenplays is fairly recent, in response to a boom in screenwriting students. Screenplays are blueprints for a movie, and the writer is more like an architect than writers of novels or poems.

- **Format**: Screenplays are written in a special format that is much easier to learn than you may think. It requires no knowledge of camera angles or the technical aspects of film (this was not always so).

- **Collaboration**: Successful screenwriting depends upon successful collaboration. No narrative form is more collaborative – unfortunately in ways in which the writer is not in control. Except in early pre-market drafts, the screenwriter *is always working for someone* and the ability and willingness to collaborate is essential.

- **Concept**: Your story concept is the first thing producers and agents respond to. When development executives buy a script from a new screenwriter, ninety percent of the time they are buying the story concept, not the writing. As you learn craft, you should write the stories you have to tell. Later, as you venture into the market, you will take a different tack, trying to conceive of stories that are highly marketable, a skill entirely distinct from writing. The ability to create marketable story ideas is probably the single most important skill.

Reality 101

Let me emphasize one of the above points: screenwriting is collaborative almost by definition. Think about that. This alone drives some writers from the form. Screenwriting is the only narrative form in which "success" means putting a product "into development" to change it.

This reminds me of a joke:

> *Two development execs meet in a hallway. One says, "Hey, what's cooking?" The second one, extremely excited, replies, "I just bought this script. It's the most perfect piece of writing I've ever seen. Characters, story, EVERYTHING about it is A-number-one. Academy award time."*
>
> *"Fantastic," says the first. "So when do you go into production?"*
>
> *"As soon as I get the rewrite."*

You write a poem, short story, or novel. You send it out hoping it will be published. It may require revisions, but typically these are minor. Even playwriting, though collaborative, focuses on realizing the writer's vision. This is seldom true of screenwriting. Once screenwriters enter collaboration, they are no longer in charge. The opinions of the producer, director, even of the major actor, are more important than the screenwriter's.

In screenwriting "writing for art's sake" is almost a contradiction in terms. In fiction, poetry, drama, or creative nonfiction the writer can choose to write as art or to write commercially. Those who choose art write to satisfy their aesthetic sensibilities. They express their own tastes, not those of an audience. Those who write to sell write primarily to please others, focusing almost completely on a particular audience's needs and expectations.

Novelist Graham Greene divided his fiction into serious work, which he called novels, and popular work, which he called entertainments. Similarly, a poet might write verse for *Reader's Digest* or serious poetry for the more exclusive market represented by poetry journals. Dorothy Parker called her poetry 'verse' because she believed it failed to reach that standard. Emily Dickinson, in contrast, is the poet-as-artist, putting her poems into a drawer, writing primarily for herself.

Screenwriting is aimed exclusively at commerce, toward pleasing an audience. The one small exception is art film directors who write their own scripts. Unless you are both a screenwriter and filmmaker, you are not writing screenplays "for art's sake."

Let's say you send out a script. A producer buys an option on it. Before taking it out to find a deal, the producer puts his or her own stamp on it, meaning the screenwriter rewrites according to the producer's taste and dictates. A star likes the script, forming an attachment to the project. You rewrite the script to satisfy the star. A director comes on board, and now the director is boss. Changes are made under his or her watchful and necessarily approving eye. All along the way, the screenwriter is rewriting to satisfy others. Unlike playwrights, novelists, or poets, screenwriters are powerless even though they initially created the story.

Another joke:

> Did you hear about the ambitious young starlet so ignorant
> of the film industry that she slept with the screenwriter?

Richard Price (*The Color of Money*) puts it bluntly in *American Screenwriters*:

> I'm just saying how things are. But creatively it's a bunch
> of shit because you put everything you have into the first
> draft. The rest is chipping away at what you did to make it
> look like everything else that's ever been done, so they can
> feel comfortable enough to put their millions of dollars
> behind it. So after you finish your first draft, you say
> goodbye, you kiss it, you wrap it in its bundle, and you just
> watch it get changed. And if you want to get it done and
> you want your name on it, you have to do the hacking. But
> you never care about it as much after the first draft.

Price usually writes after selling an idea, so his first draft is the last one he works on alone. As a beginning writer, you will write many drafts, but once you get interest in your script, as Price notes (speaking as a novelist), the story no longer is yours alone.

David Thomson, a book author who sometimes writes for the screen, commented on collaboration in "Writing for a Business Where No One Reads," published in the *Sunday New York Times* (4/1/01). He emphasizes the differences between screenwriting and "real writing":

> Yet screenwriting isn't actually writing – that needs to be
> said and allowed to sink in. Writing cannot exist without
> reading, and in the movies, the only things that are read
> are contracts, credits and subtitles.

" 'Real' writers," he points out, "never trade away the privileges of copyright, of owning their work." Screenwriters, in contrast, make a kind of Faustian deal with the devil:

> But they have made a bargain for success. Ultimately, the American picture depends on being a hit. The Writer's Guild...has to face that fact. Screenwriters can't write for the sake of words and reading. They are clever typists in a business that likes to regard all its necessary workers as properties. So nearly every screenwriter dies crushed – with a well-fed, well-maintained corpse surrounding a large soggy heart still yearning for novels, plays, poetry and respect.

Harsh words but true. The essential point is that screenplays are not literary documents but invitations to collaboration. Though you originate the process, you end up one of its least powerful members.

Producers get writers to change scripts in many ways. Screenwriter Steve Rivele (*Ali, Nixon*) put it this way (*New York Times Magazine*, 11/03/02):

> There are basically four ways producers get you to change something. The first is that they just won't turn it in to the studio. Of course, they never say it like that. They'll say, 'We just want it to be as good as possible when we turn it in.' But they mean that they won't turn it in without the changes, and because you get paid for delivering a final draft, you won't be paid until you make the changes. The second is they fire you. The third is they overwhelm you with such breathtakingly stupid suggestions that you begin to doubt your own judgment. You think, God, is it possible I'm the one not getting this? ... Finally, when they find out that you've fallen in love with the story, they can endlessly manipulate you. They know you think it's important that this actually get seen by the public. Then you're dead.

Money and Reality 101

Another misconception is that screenwriting is an easy or at least likely way to get rich. In the 1990s, the newspapers ran numerous stories about million-dollar screenplay sales. Budding writers took interest.

Dana Kennedy in the *New York Times* (Dec. 9, 2001) puts the phenomenon in context.

> "It was like this big scam," says Chris Gore, editor of the online magazine *Film Threat*. "There was all this buzz, all

these bragging rights and all these ego-driven deals. But really what happened was that screenwriting turned into an industry preying on all these people from Michigan or someplace who think they're going to come out here and write a screenplay and make $1 million overnight. It became like the lottery."

But recently the situation changed. "Screenwriters Adjust to Being Bit Players Again," to quote the title of this article. "The mid-90s gold rush that resulted in multimillion-dollar scripts (and some very bad movies) is over," Kennedy concludes.

Credits and Reality 101

Another peculiarity of the business is that good money can be made without ever seeing one's work on the screen. I've optioned six different screenplays. Not one ended up as a movie. There are more extreme examples.

In *The Oregonian* on January 8, 2002, Margie Boule interviewed Ken Nolan, writer of *Black Hawk Down*. Nolan struggled for a decade in Hollywood before selling his first script. Although this gave him income, it didn't establish him as a screenwriter. Boule picks up the story:

> Ken wrote another script that sold, and then others. Each sold for more than the one before it, but none was ever made into a movie. Ken found himself locked into a Hollywood pattern: "You have a really successful writing career, a house, a fancy car, people know who you are—but no movies ever come out."

I had a friend whose parents were convinced he was a drug dealer! How else could he have so much money and nothing concrete to show for it?

Screenwriting is unlike any reality you've ever entered. Be prepared.

Screenwriter v. Director

The director's role as a film's creative "boss" is a reality many beginners resist. If you don't like it, become a director! Become a filmmaker. You can write your own scripts, but you will have to direct them to retain any creative control. Even then, you will be working for the producer.

Stephen Gaghan, screenwriter of *Traffic*, is an Oscar-winning screenwriter-turned-director. He told the *New York Times* (Sunday, September 8, 2002) how his notion of screenwriting changed after directing *Abandon*.

...it wasn't until I became a director that I realized nobody had been listening [to me as a screenwriter]. Oh, they look as though they're listening to you, the writer, as you make the sounds we associate with speech; but really they're waiting, thinking private thoughts about fingernail colors and evening traffic on the Ventura Freeway, waiting to see if the director is listening to you. And then they listen to the director. Of course, the only way I could learn this was by becoming a director ... I don't completely agree with this system but there is a good reason nobody listens to the screenwriter: he isn't accountable. The screenwriter is like an economist or political commentator who says, 'If you don't cut interest rates right now, there will be a 3 percent decline in housing starts next April.' But nobody checks back next April. Nobody remembers or cares. Because you don't have to act on the decision, you aren't responsible for the fallout. You are an advisor, not a builder. And if 'real housing starts' decline by 20 percent and the construction industry lays off thousands – well, you still have your comfy chair and nice view out the window. For the director, it is the exact opposite. The time for theorizing is over. It is yes or no, and pretty soon you have an aesthetic. Period.

Remember it's not the screenwriter who risks pouring tens of millions of dollars into a product that might or might not turn a profit for investors. The producer hires the director as creative boss, and the screenwriter is way down the chain of command. All the same, screenwriters love to give directors an occasional reminder:

The screenwriter of a Frank Capra comedy was watching a TV interview with the great director. An awestruck reporter was heaping praise on a passage from the writer's script, and Capra explained the scene's charm by saying, "That's the Capra touch." The reporter continued gushing about parts of other Capra movies. In each case, the director's comment was, "That's the Capra touch."

The writer loaded 120 blank pages between two card stock covers, impaled this "screenplay" with brads, and mailed the package to Capra with a note: "Put the Capra touch to THIS."

Keeping the Dream Alive

Though successful movies have much in common, they also express an artist's individuality. You dream of becoming a screenwriter. You have stories no one else can tell. If you learn, if you master this craft, your imagination has to have a language that expresses those unique stories in a powerful and moving way. My goal is to give you the necessary tools.

Exercises

1. Divide a sheet of paper into two columns. In the left, list all the directors you can remember. In the right, list all the screenwriters. What does this tell you about screenwriting?

2. Do the same exercise for stage play directors and playwrights. What does this tell you about how playwrights compare with screenwriters?

3. Why are you interested in screenwriting? What are your immediate goals? As a screenwriter, what do you hope to be doing five years from now?

2

YOUR MOVIE'S CONCEPT

I began screenwriting "thinking like a playwright." It was a great mistake. I did not realize how important "concept" is in Hollywood's highly competitive arena. As a result I often struck out before I put a single word on the computer screen. My movie story concepts were not "grabbers." It was a hard lesson. I hope I can help you learn it sooner than I did.

What's It All About?

Hollywood is idea-driven, story-concept driven. Screenwriting is more a storyteller's than a writer's medium. A screenplay is not intended to be read for enjoyment but as the first step in a long process of bringing a story to film. Consequently, screenplays need to be written *simply* so the story (not the writing!) comes to the fore. Let me offer you this important advice: *don't let your writing get in the way of your story.* What an extraordinary thing to tell a writer! Novelists are encouraged to hone their facility with language and metaphor. For screenwriters, however, storytelling is central, and this requires a different set of skills.

High Concept

Late in the 1970s, according to Justin Wyatt in *High Concept: Movies and Marketing in Hollywood*, Hollywood distilled its needs down to a buzzword: *high concept*. In *How to Sell Your Idea to Hollywood*, Robert Kosberg, something of a Hollywood legend for pitching movie concepts to studios, defines it this way:

> The essence of high concept is that it is both brief and provocative. It piques the imagination and promises that big things are going to happen out of an ordinary situation. . . . The test is in whether you can describe a provocative movie in one or two lines. If someone else were to look at that one-liner and ask, But what's the movie about?, then you do not have a high concept. The next step is to breeze through a copy of *TV Guide* and read the one-liners used

to describe scheduled movies. Try to emulate the style and structure of *TV Guide* listings in executing your idea.

A movie idea is "high concept" if:

- It's easily and quickly understood by almost anyone.
- It can be explained in a sentence or two.
- It's larger than life.
- It has a clear central character facing a clear conflict.
- It's fresh but not too fresh, not risky.

You can see how a playwright's approach is seldom compatible with such stringent demands. I am used to writing stories that matter to me, and my reasons for beginning a stage play are always more personal than commercial.

In Hollywood, this approach is more typical of an independent filmmaker. As a screenwriter, you are competing with a staggering number of screenplays; concept is what immediately distinguishes one story from another.

Good Movie Concepts

A good commercial movie concept shares a number of features:

- It reveals "a world beyond the ordinary." Movies are larger than life. A good movie concept puts us in that world.
- It has universal appeal. The story embraces emotions and experiences we identify with.
- It reflects stories we've seen in movies before. A common high concept pitch takes the form, "*Tootsie* meets *Kramer v. Kramer*" (*Mrs. Doubtfire*). Despite plenty of disappointing clones and sequels, Hollywood producers strive to build on success, and good concepts can combine elements of earlier successful movies.
- It implies a dramatic situation. "The First Lady is kidnapped and held for ransom by terrorists." We immediately know the situation and what has to be done to resolve it.
- It gives us privileged "behind the scenes" information. The movie is extraordinary because it introduces us into a world ordinarily restricted to us.
- It suggests good roles. Hollywood is star-driven. If you can create stories stars want to be in, you have done a lot of your work.

- It's easily placed in one of the major genres: drama, comedy, action/adventure, suspense/thriller, epic, sci-fi, romance, detective/crime, horror, western. Or, in some combination or more specific version of them: romantic comedy, erotic thriller, coming-of-age comedy, or epic historical drama.

Genre is especially important in business-focused Hollywood. Ask yourself, which shelf will they put my movie's video on when it's released?

Genre

Let's examine genre more closely:

- *Drama*: Something of a catchall, a story is "drama" when it is serious and doesn't fit easily into another genre. Drama is usually character-driven but strong subplots help its commercial appeal.
- *Comedy*: A comedy makes you laugh. The romantic comedy has become a popular and important genre in its own right, a romance with a light-hearted touch and a happy ending.
- *Action/adventure*: Lots of action scenes and often special effects, a plot-driven story with a clear (often super) hero who wins against great odds.
- *Suspense/thriller*: A story driven by "what happens next?" A mystery that keeps us on the edges of our seats. Often the hero is an ordinary person in extraordinary circumstances. There can be "romantic thrillers" like *North By Northwest* and "erotic thrillers" like *Body Heat*.
- *Epic*: Larger than life stories that embrace great, often historical, settings. *Titanic* can be called an "epic romance."
- *Science fiction*: A story set in another time, place, universe, often with supernatural or advanced technological elements. Often crossbred with another genre.
- *Romance*: Boy-meets-girl love stories, treated more seriously than in a romantic comedy.
- *Detective/crime*: Related to suspense/thriller but driven by a detective or cop hero.
- *Horror*: Movies with monsters or un-humanlike creatures that scare the hell out of you. Crazed humans also qualify.
- *Western*: Cowboys, horses, the old West or the values and heroes of the old West in a more modern setting. Clear good guys and bad guys.

Examples of Movie Concepts

Let's look at some good movie concepts. A concept's pithy one- or two-sentence expression is called a *logline*.

- Jaws in space: *Aliens*.
- A hard-boiled cop becomes a kindergarten teacher: *Kindergarten Cop*.
- What if a baby could talk? *Look Who's Talking*.
- A male actor cross-dresses to get work: *Tootsie*.
- A teenager hacks into the Pentagon's computer: *War Games*.
- The President of the U.S. falls in love: *American President*.
- A boy befriends an alien, then helps him escape from scientists and return home: *E.T.*
- A Nazi tracker discovers Hitler has been cloned: *Boys from Brazil*.
- A white woman discovers her daughter is black: *Secrets and Lies*.
- A male comic book artist falls in love with a lesbian: *Chasing Amy*.

Two movie concepts created considerable "buzz" and even a bidding war in 1998. In one, a homeless man lives in the Statue of Liberty. In the other, number eleven on the FBI's Most Wanted List is so angry at missing the top ten he eliminates everyone ahead of him on the list.

The latter is more detailed, but both quickly present dramatic situations that are clearly filmic. "High concept" creates an idea quickly recognized to "be a movie."

Consider this article from *Variety* (May 6, 1999):

HOLLYWOOD (Variety)—Off just an e-mail pitch from an unknown French screenwriter, producer Larry Thompson (*And the Beat Goes On: The Sonny and Cher Story*) has locked up the film and TV rights to Internet thriller *Murder.com*.

Thompson signed a low six-figure deal with Philip Devereaux, the 23-year-old *Murder* scribe, without any preliminary discussions or read-throughs.

Murder tells the story of a French serial killer who brandishes a human virus for a weapon, and torments his victims through e-mail.

Thompson, who has no clue how Devereaux managed to grab hold of his e-mail address, has flown to France for a first-time meeting with the uncredited writer.

No production date has been set for the project.

It almost seems the producer bought the title of the script, "Murder.com," which indeed is a natural. When a producer "turns on" to a concept, things can happen very quickly. The urgency, buying "without any preliminary discussions or read-throughs," suggests how badly the producer wanted this project.

You can read about recent script deals in trade publications like *Variety* and on the Internet. In September 2000, the following pitch sold—one of those ideas that makes you slap your head and say, "Why didn't I think of that?"

THE DOCTOR AND THE DOORMAN

A woman surgeon can't get dates because she is too bright and well employed; a man can't get dates because he is only a doorman. When they meet, she pretends to be a 2nd grade teacher and he pretends to be a stockbroker. Now they are falling in love but are afraid to reveal the truth to one another.

Loglines

Learning to write these one-line concepts or "loglines" does two things: helps you focus on your story's spine or foundation and helps you market your script afterward.

Many loglines follow this pattern:

CHARACTER + ACTION + GOAL

"A boy (character) befriends an alien (action) and helps him return home" (goal).

"A man (character) cross-dresses as a nanny (action) to see his kids (goal).

Loglines can be improved with implied or stated conflict: "A lonely boy befriends an alien and rescues him from the government so he can return home." "An estranged husband cross-dresses as a nanny to see his kids despite his wife's objections."

Loglines are powerful tools because their brevity forces you to think about the spine of your story.

Examples of Loglines

You will find a good resource for tight loglines is the movie schedule at Turner Classic Movies. A few examples:

- *Where Danger Lives* (1950) A psychopath draws her doctor into her murderous schemes.
- *Day of the Evil Gun* (1968) A gunman tries to control a vengeful farmer whose wife has been kidnapped.
- *One Million Years B.C.* (1966) A rebellious caveman leaves his tribe in search of a better life.
- *Grease* (1978) A prim Australian exchange student falls for a high-school gang leader.
- *Cat on a Hot Tin Roof* (1958) A dying plantation owner tries to help his alcoholic son solve his problems.

Note how succinctly the spine of each is expressed.

Is High Concept Necessary?

High concept can be disturbing in that it seems to reduce movies to a formula, gutting the very creativity and imagination most writers take pride in. If you believe this, try coming up with a high-concept idea yourself. It's a lot harder to come up with blockbuster ideas than you may think.

The downside to Hollywood's attraction to "high concept" is that sometimes writing quality gets lost in the shuffle. Consider these startling words from literary agent Bob Bookman, quoted in Linda Stuart's *Getting Your Script Through the Hollywood Maze*:

> I've read a lot of scripts that sold in the half-million to million-dollar range, and it really depressed me.... I represented a screenwriting team and sold two or three scripts of theirs for a lot of money. They were all very high concept-driven scripts that, in my opinion, were not very well written. Those were the highest numbers that I got for spec scripts, and it depressed me a lot.

On the other hand, not every movie has a high concept. Even if we can usually reduce a movie's idea to several sentences, many movies are quieter and more character-driven, particularly those made by independent filmmakers outside the studio system.

Consider the loglines of two of my own scripts that have been optioned:

> A woman tries to stop her teenage daughter from making the same mistakes she did—and with the same man: *Ruby's Tune*.

A Vietnam war draft dodger accepts President Carter's pardon to return home and make peace with his father, a World War II hero: *The Pardon*.

High concept? Yes, the dramatic situation is immediately understood; and no, these are not blockbuster ideas. Several producers have referred to them as ideas for "good little movies." This, by the way, is usually pejorative.

Concepts for Learning v. Concepts for Selling

One of the first things you must do is define your territory. Do you want to write studio blockbusters or "good little movies" for smaller producers?

Many of the same principles apply, and you can do both simultaneously with different scripts. But making a choice—or at least being aware of the difference —is important, so you know your market.

Choosing your movie concept is less critical in the beginning of your career because you can learn craft with a less marketable script. You should begin by writing stories you feel passionate about, stories you can't help writing. Because you are going to have to market your concept as a spec script, you need to learn craft before anything else.

Your Project's Concept

Now it's your turn. Write the concept for the project you are going to develop through this course. Write it as a logline—you'll be filling the story out later as you work on a paradigm chart, a step outline, and a treatment.

Spend some time choosing the concept. Come up with five before you select one you'll stick with. Use the template CHARACTER + ACTION + GOAL with implied conflict to focus on the story's spine. Later you can revise the logline wearing your "ad man" hat. Your goal now is story clarity.

Exercises

1. Start a Movie Journal. Keep track of the movies you see and try to express the stories in succinct loglines.
2. Start a Screenplay Ideas Journal to keep track of your own ideas. Again, expressed as succinct loglines.
3. List a dozen or more movies you admire. Mark the "high concept" stories. What percentage of these movies depend on high concept? Also note genres, and in this way, you will begin to identify your screenwriting territory. Will you be more comfortable writing "big" movies or "small" ones, high concept stories or more intimate, character-driven ones? If you are more attracted to a specific genre, these may be the kinds of stories you should write.

3

Finding Your Writing Method

You have a concept you like—let's say it's: *The First Lady is kidnapped and held for ransom by terrorists.*

Now what?

Different Strokes

One of the difficult things about teaching writing, or any of the arts, is that any teaching methodology implies a "right way" of writing. I'm not referring to common elements embodied in any good screenplay. I mean how you write–your writing method.

William Faulkner reportedly said, "Writing can't be taught—but it can be learned." I'm inclined to agree.

Even established screenwriters find they begin different projects differently:

> "It's been different every single time," notes Jim Cash, who wrote *Top Gun*. "You just write. You start with something, though. You start with what you feel to be the heart of the story, one way or another. Sometimes the heart of a story is a character, sometimes it's a situation, sometimes it's a personal story of a character. When I say a situation, I mean it's something so unique that you can make a story out of it. It's just different every time" (from *American Screenwriters*).

Unlike the market's plentiful "screenplay gurus" who claim to know the best method for writing commercially successful screenplays, I think a good teacher is like a guide: someone who has been exposed to a variety of approaches, who can suggest ways of getting from here to there.

The fact is, all our creative styles differ. I have friends who do an extraordinary amount of "left-brained" analysis before they ever begin to write. They do things like:

- write character profiles
- write a step outline
- draw a paradigm chart
- build character vocabulary books
- build plot point sequences
- build character arcs

If you don't know what these are, you will soon enough. If they make sense to you, incorporate them into your screenwriting process. The point I'm making is that I know other writers, myself included, who do none of these things. This is not to say we don't plan—we do—but some writers like to jump into a story immediately. Harold Pinter likes to put two characters in a room to see if anything interesting happens. Planning, in other words, means different things to different people.

Tree People v. Forest People

To broadly generalize, there seem to be two kinds of writers: the tree people and the forest people.

Tree people prefer starting with the small picture; forest people with the big picture. Tree people plan the details before they begin. Forest people jump in sooner, trusting in the dynamics of creation to make decisions about detail along the way.

A forest person can be turned off by a teacher with a tree person's approach and vice-versa. A friend of mine who teaches playwriting requires students to fill out notebooks of character biographies. I would rebel against this – it would dissipate the very energy I use for writing. By the time I finished such an exercise, I would have lost interest in the project.

Identifying your natural writing method will allow you to focus on certain sections in this book that will make less sense to writers of the opposite style.

Tree People: Everything in Its Place

Today, most screenwriting books, methodologies, and systems are aimed at tree people. Indeed, the usual development process of moving a film story from concept to script to screen involves the careful step-by-step planning at the heart of how tree people do things.

If you're a tree person, you'll be right at home because most of what is written about the craft is aimed at you. You'll be encouraged to further develop what you're already doing:

- outlining before you write
- making notes about your characters and story line
- knowing your story inside and out before you start writing it

As a tree person, you're going to face a dizzying assortment of "paradigms" urging you to structure your story this way or that, and you'll want to become familiar with most of them to discover which resonate with you.

You also might want to invest in a box of index cards. Index cards lend themselves to making a step outline, a functional, left-brained approach to story development. Colored markers can be used to trace things like plot points on the cards.

Not all tree people work with index cards. Planning is the key to a tree person's method, but Ron Bass, who wrote *Black Widow* and *Rain Man*, does it this way (quoted in *American Screenwriters*):

> "I don't work from index cards. I write screenplays—and novels as well—from a story outline. I don't like to write any scene until I think I know where everything is going, because everything I do is informed by that. Of course, the outline may change radically as I go. But just to kick off and say, here's an interesting first scene, now where do I go from there? Some people are very successful at that, but it's not my style."

Forest People: Creation As Discovery

Forest people can feel lonely in Hollywood. The left-brained approach that appeals to tree people is a thriving cottage industry. Buzzwords are everywhere: paradigm, plot point, character arc, and most of all—structure, structure, structure!

Not everyone rides this bandwagon. Some successful screenwriters stand apart. DiAnne Olson Wosep interviewed Chris McQuarrie, writer of *The Usual Suspects*, for an online magazine, and he offered some confessions from a forest person:

> Tell your story. Rules lead to formula, Formula leads nowhere. One of the first meetings I took after *Suspects* was sold, a development exec said to me:
>
> "You are so bold. You broke the big rule. You used flashbacks and THEY WORKED!!!"
>
> I never went to school to learn I couldn't do that. There are no bad conventions. There is only bad writing and the attempt to salvage it with conventions.
>
> Again with *Jaws*. How many acts in that? How many arcs? How many stories?

Form is nonsense. Only the story matters. Trust it to tell itself as you see it. After the first 20 pages, a story should be moving YOU along.

Another "forest person," Bruce Joel Rubin, wrote *Ghost*:

"I'm never intentional. I'm totally intuitive. I don't understand structure, at least in the academic sense. If you asked me today what a denouement is, I cannot tell you. I don't know my first act break from my second act break. Now, granted, I have to go back and identify them with the help of producers and directors, but I don't write that way. I just write from the gut, let it come out, and it tends to shape itself." (from *American Screenwriters*).

Joe Eszterhas, who established himself in the 1980s and 1990s as the highest paid screenwriter in Hollywood history, was asked whether he worked within a three-act structure.

"No, I just start writing. And sometimes I don't know where it's going to go. That's when it gets really exciting to me, when I don't know how it's going to go, because it's not locked in, it's not set." (from *American Screenwriters*)

I.A.L. Diamond (*The Private Life of Sherlock Holmes*, *The Apartment*), says, "I'm afraid that if I get it worked out too well, then I'm going to find the writing boring. I'd rather just have a few signposts and leave a lot of wide-open spaces, so things can happen when I'm writing. I don't like to have it down too cold or too well figured out before I start, because I think some of the excitement and enthusiasm goes out of it" (*American Screenwriters*).

Still another forest person, author Truman Capote, wrote a number of memorable television dramas.

"I invariably have the illusion that the whole play of a story, its start and middle and finish, occur in my mind simultaneously – that I'm seeing it in one flash. But in the working-out, the writing-out, infinite surprises happen. Thank God, because surprise, the twist, the phrase that comes at the right moment out of nowhere, is the unexpected dividend, the joyful little push that keeps a writer going. At one time I used to keep notebooks with outlines for stories. But I found doing this somehow deadened the idea in my imagination. If the notion is good enough, if it truly belongs to YOU, then you can't forget it ... it will haunt you till it's written." (*Paris Review*, Summer 1988)

Marshall Brickman made this comment about working on *Annie Hall* with Woody Allen.

> "The first script...was much more episodic, tangential, and novelistic....It didn't work for us. We started to become interested in the love story between Woody and the Keaton character, which was all over the place. We cut and pasted to make the love story more important, and the structure emerged. The material was telling us what to do." (*American Screenwriters*)

The notion that the story impels the writer is a pure forest person sentiment. I hope most writers get to experience this sensation because nothing equals the magic of characters rushing forward with your story, begging you to keep up.

This is not to say your characters always lead you directly or infallibly to the most engaging story. Nonetheless, most writers experience this process at one time or another. Forest people thrive on it and go with the flow; tree people tend to get nervous when their step outline has defined a different progression.

Forest people aren't afraid of the unknown. They trust they will discover what they need to know along the way. They are willing to delay using the analytical part of the brain until they're rewriting.

Consider character biographies. A strict tree person wants to know everything possible about the major characters: their favorite foods and colors, their secrets, their most embarrassing moments. They want to know before they start writing. Consequently, they often write character biographies or fill out the kind of forms contained in story development software like Collaborator.

As a borderline forest person, I don't write character biographies. This "failure" can result in amusing incidents. Once, in rehearsal with my best-known play, *Christmas at the Juniper Tavern*, an actor asked me about his character. "What was Rex's favorite subject in high school?" he wanted to know.

I couldn't answer exactly, though I was sure Rex didn't like mathematics, physics, or chemistry. Maybe shop or P.E., I thought.

"What do you think?" I asked the actor. He thought a while.

"This is probably way off base but—I think he doesn't like any class for the subject matter but for the teacher. I think he had a history teacher he really liked."

Looking like the most surprised playwright in America, I said, "You're absolutely right! That's incredible."

The actor beamed, empowered by his sudden insight. We were both happy.

Having filled out a form on Rex's character before I wrote the play wouldn't have helped me one iota in this encounter nor improved the wonderful performance given by the actor. The actors, more than the script, communicate to the audience, which is why I call my playwriting classes "the art of writing for actors."

Forest people think tree people get lost in the detail and miss the fun of discovery. Forest people put off using their left brains as long as possible. They'd rather analyze things after they have a script.

What Is Your Natural Writing Method?

Are you a tree person or a forest person? You probably already know which way you lean. Through the rest of this book you will have special instructions tailored to your inclination. Writers of the opposite persuasion will go elsewhere to cover the same material. (Of course, you can read both tree and forest material. This will involve some duplication, which is not the worst environment for learning new concepts.)

The Writing Method Preference Test

If you're still uncertain whether you are a tree or forest person, I offer a very unscientific test that may help.

Choose one answer for each question.

1. When grocery shopping you write a list: A. usually, B. seldom, C. never?
2. When giving a dinner party you write down your menu: A. usually, B. seldom, C. never.
3. Planning a two-week vacation, you choose a specific itinerary ahead of time: A. usually, B. seldom, C. never?
4. In a strange city you find brochures in your hotel describing the local attractions. Do you: A. Read them and list what you want to see, B. Read them but don't make a list, C. Don't read them at all?
5. You are camping in an unfamiliar area. Do you: A. study a map, find campsites, and write down their names, B. glance at the map but don't make a list, C. just take off, figuring you'll find a campsite along the way?

Tabulating Results

Count 2 points for each A answer, 1 point for each B answer, and 0 points for each C answer.

- 10-8 points: tree person
- 7-6 points: leaning toward tree person
- 5 points: borderline
- 4-3 points: leaning toward forest person
- 2-0 points: forest person

Writing with a Partner

If you are a tree person, you also might consider writing with a partner. (I can't imagine how forest people would do this.) I have twice collaborated on a screenplay behaving like a tree person, and the experience was better than I anticipated.

The advantage of a partner is the dialogue or debate that begins immediately about script concept and development. I remember writing a step outline on a chalkboard with a partner—what a high-energy experience that was!

In left-brained activity, sometimes two heads really are better than one. Screenwriting—especially in early story development—lends itself to the give and take of working with a writing partner. Actually writing the script was another matter. My partner and I had such different writing styles that this important part of the process was less successful. Perhaps two scripts should be developed at once, both partners participating in story development but only one writing or drafting the script.

At any rate, because screenwriting lends itself to collaboration, you might want to consider this option.

Exercises

1. Think about past writing projects you feel good about. Where did the ideas come from? How much planning did you do before actually writing? Was your method closer to a tree person or a forest person?
2. Think about a past writing project you had trouble with, even abandoned. What was the source of the problem? Would more planning have helped? If so, what kept you from doing the necessary planning?
3. Do you finish most writing projects? If not, why do you stop? Would more planning help?

4

SCREENPLAY FORMAT

Before beginning to write, students must learn correct screenplay format. This sometimes causes more stress than necessary. Screenplay format is pretty straightforward—except that the conventional style is always changing.

It is useful to look at formerly acceptable formats out of fashion today. Older formats included camera angles and other visual concerns now considered the province of the director. Today's format, a more general "master scene approach" to storytelling, includes only a scene's basic visual locations.

Screenplay software is available to format your script as you write, and serious screenwriters should own such a program. If you can't afford it, add-ons and templates to your word processing program will also work.

Spec Scripts v. Shooting Scripts

First, let's go over the rudiments. Screenplay format can be initially confusing because students seldom see examples of what we call spec scripts, scripts written "on speculation" and subsequently marketed. The published scripts we commonly see are "shooting" scripts, different in several ways because they are the product of collaboration between writer, director, producer, and possibly even actors.

Let's compare a shooting script with a spec script. Here is a sequence from the shooting script of Magnolia:

```
39. INT. SMILING PEANUT BAR—NIGHT

CAMERA moves in on a young woman CLAUDIA
(20s) sitting alone, a bit drunk. A
vaguely creepy looking MIDDLE AGED GUY
(40s) takes a seat next to her.

               MIDDLE AGED GUY
     Hey.
```

```
                    CLAUDIA
          Hi.

                                   CUT TO:

40. INT. CLAUDIA'S APARTMENT—LATER

A series of quick shots where the
following happens: CLAUDIA and the MIDDLE
AGED GUY stumble into her apartment.
CAMERA DOLLIES in quick as she snorts a
line of coke from her coffee table ...
TILT up and PAN over to him.

                    MIDDLE AGED GUY
          So?

                                   CUT TO:

41. INT. CLAUDIA'S BEDROOM—MOMENTS LATER

CAMERA DOLLIES in quick as they're having
sex. He's on top of her, she's below,
CAMERA lands in a CLOSE UP of her face as
she gets through the experience ... CAMERA
moves up and past her, finds a reflection of
the TELEVISION in a picture frame on her
wall ...

                                   DISSOLVE TO:
```

This is not acceptable spec script format. Compare this with the version rewritten as a current spec script:

```
   INT. SMILING PEANUT BAR—NIGHT

A young woman, CLAUDIA (20s), is sitting
alone, a bit drunk.
A vaguely creepy MIDDLE AGED GUY (40s)
sits next to her.

                    MIDDLE AGED GUY
          Hey.

                    CLAUDIA
          Hi.

INT. CLAUDIA'S APARTMENT—NIGHT

Claudia and the middle aged guy stumble
into her apartment.
```

```
She heads straight for the coffee table,
where she snorts a line of coke.
                 MIDDLE AGED GUY
          So?

INT. CLAUDIA'S BEDROOM—NIGHT

They're having sex. The middle-aged guy is
on top.

Her expression reveals she's just getting
through it.

A picture on the wall reflects the
television screen.
```

Note the absence of camera angles or even references to a camera. All of the images in the shooting script are retained in the spec script but not information about how the images should be shot. The spec script simply tells the story, letting the director figure out how to shoot it.

The Elements of Screenplay Format

Format boils down to this:

```
FADE IN:

INT. CHARLES' OFFICE—NIGHT

CHARLES, 60s, sits at a computer. Looking
over his shoulder is JOHN, 20s, one of his
students.
                 CHARLES
          This format stuff isn't as hard as
          you think it is. There are a few
          simple rules, and all you have to
          do is follow them.

                 JOHN
          What are the rules?

                 CHARLES
          For most of your writing, you'll
          be using only four format
          elements. Watch the computer
          screen.
Charles begins typing at the keyboard.
John moves in closer.
```

```
The following appears ON THE COMPUTER
SCREEN:

"THIS IS WHERE A SLUGLINE GOES"

"This is where an action line goes."

          "CHARACTER NAME HERE"
     "Dialogue here."

Charles stops typing and looks at John.

          CHARLES
     See how easy it is?
```

The Four Basic Elements

Let's review this.

You seldom need more than four format elements to tell the story with a professional look:

- the slugline
- the action area
- the character name
- the dialogue

THE SLUGLINE

The slugline, always in caps, identifies the shot. In the current "master scene" approach most sluglines will begin with INT. for an interior location or EXT. for exterior.

Following INT. or EXT., the place is identified: for example, INT. BEDROOM. If we need to first establish a broader context, it might look like this: INT. JOE'S HOUSE—BEDROOM. We move from the general to the specific here—for example, we do *not* write INT. BEDROOM—JOE'S HOUSE.

Following location, time of day is indicated, almost always DAY or NIGHT. If something more specific is required (such as Afternoon) – it usually isn't – indicate this in the action area or in parentheses, for example, DAY (AFTERNOON).

So, a full slugline: INT. JOE'S HOUSE—BEDROOM—NIGHT. After establishing we are in Joe's house, subsequent sluglines can drop this broader location of place. A sequence of scenes may look like this:

INT. JOE'S HOUSE—BEDROOM—NIGHT

INT. DINING ROOM—NIGHT

INT. KITCHEN—NIGHT

EXT. BACK PORCH—NIGHT

Some writers drop DAY or NIGHT once established in the scene sequence, but I discourage taking shortcuts with sluglines. I recommend designating the time in each slugline because assistant directors usually use sluglines to make the daily shooting schedule rather than using the script's page sequence. If all sluglines are self-sufficient, the assistant director won't have to struggle backward through the script to find the needed information. Be a good collaborator!

Sluglines are flush with your left margin. A good place to set the left margin is an inch in, about 17 spaces.

THE ACTION AREA

Action lines are also flush left. The important thing to remember is you need to surround action with lots of white space. Consider this action description, from James Cameron's *Aliens*, written in an older format style.

```
EXT. COLONY COMPLEX

The town is a cluster of bunkerlike metal
and concrete buildings connected by
conduits. Neon signs throw garish colors
across the vaultlike walls, advertising
bars and other businesses. It looks like a
sodden cross between the Krupps munitions
works and a truck stop casino in the Nevada
boondocks. Huge-wheeled tractors crawl
toadlike in the rutted "street" and vanish
down rampways to underground garages.

ANGLE ON THE CONTROL BLOCK, the largest
structure. It resembles vaguely the super-
structure of an aircraft carrier, a flying
bridge. VISIBLE across a half kilometer of
barren heath, b.g., is the massive complex
of the nearest ATMOSPHERE PROCESSOR,
looking like a power plant bred with an
active volcano. Its fiery glow pulses in the
low cloud cover like a steel mill.
```

Compare this with:

```
EXT. COLONY COMPLEX - NIGHT

The town is a cluster of bunkerlike metal
and concrete buildings connected by
conduits.

Neon signs throw garish colors across the
vaultlike walls, advertising bars and
```

```
other businesses. It looks like a sodden
cross between the Krupps munitions works
and a truck stop casino in the Nevada
boondocks.

Huge-wheeled tractors crawl toadlike
in the rutted "street" and vanish down
rampways to underground garages.

THE CONTROL BLOCK is the largest
structure. It resembles vaguely the
superstructure of an aircraft carrier...a
flying bridge.

Visible across a half kilometer of barren
heath is the massive complex of the
nearest ATMOSPHERE PROCESSOR, looking like
a power plant bred with an active volcano.

Its fiery glow pulses in the low cloud
cover like a steel mill.
```

Because white space breaks up the action, the second version is much easier to read. You can break up the action even more. A writer friend who has sold action/adventure scripts to Columbia will not write an action section longer than five lines before starting a new paragraph and prefers keeping action paragraphs at three lines and under.

We drop ANGLE ON from current format style because it's redundant. The fact you've isolated "The Control Block is the largest structure" in its own paragraph is sufficient to emphasize you are "angling on" it. Omitting ANGLE ON is another example of removing all reference to the camera.

The White Space Test

Screenplays are not so much read as skimmed, at least in your first "reading"—which may be your only reading. I once saw a producer pick up a script and flip the pages quickly – not reading – just watching the print rush by. "Not enough white space," he said. He tossed the unread script into the reject pile.

By submitting a spec script, you are competing with hundreds of other screenplays usually being read by a harried, underpaid reader who gets paid *per script*. Imagine being a reader for a studio or production company. On your desk are 100 scripts demanding attention. How slowly and carefully would you read?

You the writer have your first five or ten pages to "hook" the reader. Without lots of white space, your script will be physically difficult to read in a rush (i.e., "skimmed"), another excuse to toss it.

Making Scripts Vertical

At the 2002 Screenwriting Expo in Los Angeles, where I was on the faculty, speaker after speaker urged beginning screenwriters to make their scripts "vertical." What does this mean?

Reading is a horizontal exercise. We begin at the left of the page, read across to the right, drop down a line and repeat the horizontal sweep.

The screenplay, as we've said, is not a literary document, but an invitation to a long journey toward a competed film, a blueprint to be skimmed.

What is easier to skim, dense paragraphs with long complex sentences or snappy sentences in short paragraphs? Why? Because the eye, seeking information, travels more quickly down the page. Vertical writing allows potential producers to skim the story, learning the characters (hence possible actors), genre, and probable budget.

Let's look at a paragraph from a student script:

```
Derek is walking across campus. All over,
students read copies of the official campus
newspaper and Derek's magazine. One girl,
ANNA KABIS, laughs hysterically. She is
young and beautiful. Derek stops and
stares at her. A friend of Anna reads over
her shoulder, a look of shock on her face.
```

The writing is good: clear, simple sentences. However, the verticality is poor. Let's make this passage vertical:

```
Derek is walking across campus.
All over, students read copies of the
official campus newspaper and Derek's
magazine.
One girl, ANNA KABIS, laughs hysterically.
She is young and beautiful.
Derek stops and stares at her.
A friend of Anna reads over her shoulder,
a look of shock on her face.
```

Notice how much easier it is to skim? The eye races vertically down the page, rather than slowly across.

There's a hidden advantage in this for the writer. By isolating paragraphs this way, the writer is implicitly directing the movie! Each short paragraph suggests a new shot: a wide shot of students, close on Anna, back to Derek, back to Anna. Writers, forbidden to direct the movie, can influence the flow of images by suggesting new shots in new paragraphs.

The vertical script is like a long strip of film passing in front of the eyes. Adding verticality to your script has no down side.

Remember that published screenplays are terrible models for the beginning screenwriter. They lack verticality because *they are not spec scripts*. Professional screenwriters sell their *ideas* first, then write. Once a script is regarded as an investment it will be read no matter how verbose and literary.

As I said, don't let your writing get in the way of your story. And don't let formatting keep it from being read. Never forget that Hollywood is story-driven, and in a hurry.

More About the Action Area

This is not an easy adventure you're embarking on! You need to learn many things before you pack into the mountains for that long climb. Here is some more about writing in the action area.

The first time character names appear in the action element, they are capitalized. Afterward, they are written normally, with only the first letter capitalized.

The action area has picked up one additional burden in the current format: parenthetical descriptions have fallen from fashion. For example:

Old Style

```
          JOE (angrily)
     Damn it, that's not right!
```

Current Style

```
   Joe slams a book down on the desk.
          JOE
     Damn it, that's not right!
```

In other words, instead of labeling an emotion and enclosing it parentheses, demonstrate emotion through an action or describe an action that communicates it.

FORMATTING THE CHARACTER NAME
The character name is indented 43 spaces (26 from the margin set at 17) and always capitalized.

FORMATTING DIALOGUE
Dialogue starts at 28 spaces (11 from margin at 17).

Summary

Standard tab settings for format are:

- 17: Left margin
- 28: Dialogue
- 35: Parenthetical directions (not in fashion)
- 43: Character name
- 66: Transitional instructions (CUT TO:, etc.)(not in fashion today)
- 72: Page number (page numbers have a period after them: 77.)
- 75: Right margin (right margins are not justified)

Font

Screenplays are submitted in 12-point Courier or New Courier. Nothing else. This is important.

Other Considerations

The four basic elements—slugline, action, character, and dialogue—are all you need to write in today's "master scene" format. Here are a few other things to consider.

- Cover, brads, title page: Nothing fancy! Bind your script with card stock in the same color as a file folder.
- Bind the script using two brads. Punch three holes in the script but only two in the cardstock.
- On the title page use a simple format, centered, about 2/5 down the page from the top: NAME OF SCREENPLAY by Your Name. Near the bottom, flush left or flush right, put your address and phone number or your agent's name, address and phone number.

That's it. No fancy colors, no WGA number on the script, no illustrations, no colored paper.

The first page: Begin flush left with FADE IN:

Double space and write your first slugline. Note the following spaces between elements:

- single space between character and dialogue; within action paragraph; within dialogue paragraph.
- double space at end of action paragraph or element (to another action paragraph, or new element such as character or slugline); at end of dialogue; at end of slugline.

- optional triple space (instead of double space) before each new slugline. (Start with double spacing. If your script is too short, change to triple to add pages.)

Page numbers: The first page is unnumbered. Number the remaining pages at their tops, flush right, with a period after the number, i.e., 23.

Scenes moving rapidly inside and outside: sometimes it is awkward to follow action that moves quickly inside and outside. Use this: INT./EXT. JOE'S BARN—DAY.

Montage or a series of shots: Use this format:

```
A SERIES OF SHOTS—JOHN AND MARY AT THE
BEACH
They build sand castles.
They fly a kite.
They race to the water.
They swim and have a water fight.
```

Flashbacks: Use this format:

```
INT. JOE'S HOUSE—CELLAR—NIGHT (FLASHBACK)
```

Insert: Now out of fashion, this was a cutaway shot to get close on something small. Today just describe the object in its own paragraph. The director will decide how to shoot it.

Establishing shot: The slugline ESTABLISHING SHOT is out of fashion. Do something like this instead:

```
EXT. WASHINGTON D.C.—DAY
The famous landmarks rise majestically
under a bright sun.
```

Sounds: Important sounds can be capitalized. "They hear the CRASH of glass in the other room." Even this is being dropped by many writers.

Telephone conversation: There are three ways to format a phone conversation, depending on how many parties we see and hear.

- If we hear only one person:

```
                JOE
        Did I wake you?...I'm sorry....I said,
        I'm sorry!
```

- If we hear both parties but only see one:

```
                    JOE
          Did I wake you?

                    MARY (filtered)
          That's all right.
```

In this case, we only see Joe on screen.

- If we hear and see both parties:

```
INTERCUT PHONE CONVERSATION—JOE'S BEDROOM
/MARY'S BEDROOM

                    JOE
          Did I wake you?

                    MARY
          That's all right.
```

Sometimes you can do this more efficiently within the context of the story this way:

```
INT. JOE'S BEDROOM—NIGHT
Joe dials a number.
INT. MARY'S BEDROOM—NIGHT
She answers the phone.
INTERCUT
```
           [and the conversation as before]

Passing of time: in student scripts, I often see fiction devices such as, "An hour later, Tom is still watching television." This is the way to pass time in a screenplay:

```
INT. TOM'S HOUSE—LIVING ROOM—NIGHT
Tom is watching television.
INT. TOM'S HOUSE—LIVING ROOM—NIGHT—LATER
And still watching TV an hour later.
```

Here "an hour" is not a significant —we really mean "later." But if it is, then the audience must know this, and the second slugline above becomes:

```
SUPER: "An hour later"
INT. TOM'S HOUSE—LIVING ROOM—NIGHT
He is still watching television.
```

"SUPER" is short for superimposed on screen and we use it when we put "writing" on the screen. Both SUPER and the more complete SUPER ON SCREEN are used. Sometimes TITLE CARD also is used.

Special effects: don't use FX (visual) or SFX (sound), just describe the action.

Camera directions and angles: None. I repeat: none. You are not the director. This means no CUT TO: and no ANGLE ON, both of which were common in previous styles.

Continueds: This convention is no longer used. See the exception below, with more.

More: If a character's dialogue is continued onto the next page, format like this:

```
              JOE
        I'm not done here!

              (MORE)
```
---page break---
```
              JOE (cont'd)
        You also have a lousy sense of
        humor.
```

Overlapping dialogue: One of the rare uses today of parentheticals:

```
              JOE
        You couldn't tell a joke if your
        life depended on it.

              FRANK (overlapping)
        I don't have to take this.
```

Character off screen: If Joe in the dining room is on camera, talking to Mary in the kitchen, whom we don't see, the format is as follows:

```
            JOE
Honey, would you bring in the
wine?

        MARY (O.S.)
Red or white?
```

Some writers use O.C. for "off camera." Generally O.S. is for film and O.C. for television.

Narrative voice-over: If a narrator is telling your story, format as follows:

```
EXT. LOS ANGELES—FREEWAY—DAY

Bumper-to-bumper traffic on a sweltering,
smoggy day.

            JOE (V.O.)
They call it the City of Angels.
The Chamber of Commerce will tell
you how the sun's always shining
and you can pick fruit off the
trees right in your own backyard.
```

This should cover the majority of format situations. When in doubt, use common sense and the above examples as a guideline.

TV Formats

You can write MOWs (movies of the week) using standard screenplay format.

Writing for sitcoms and other specialized TV shows is beyond the scope of this book. Your best source for this is the Internet.

Software for Screenwriters

If you are serious about screenwriting, I recommend that you purchase one of the specialized programs that format your script as you write. Top-notch programs also provide scene breakdowns, permit an interface with an index card outlining program, do spelling checks and instant reformatting, and much more.

Software programs fall into two general categories: "stand alone" specialized word processors for screenplays; and specialized tools for screenwriters, such as story development tools.

The Whole Enchilada

There are half a dozen such programs on the market. The four full-fledged programs I like the best do all the basics well (format, create character lists, etc.) but have different features.

- Hollywood Screenplay (formerly Movie Master for Windows). I like the highlighting tools for locating and easily finding plot points for a quick overview of structure. Contact info: *http://www.ballisticware.com.* Underselling its more powerful competitors, I recommend Hollywood Screenplay as one of the best bargains.

- Movie Magic (formerly ScriptThing for Windows). I like the index-card interface, which automatically transfers index card sluglines to the script. A great tool for tree people! Contact info: *http://www.scriptperfection.com/* (800) 450-9450.

- Sophocles. The latest of the four programs introduces a new kind of interface, splitting the screen vertically, an outline on the left and a script on the right. I confess I've fallen in love with this software, which is competitively priced, and Sophocles is the program I regularly write with. See *http://www.sophocles. net.*

- Final Draft. Perhaps the most popular screenwriting program. For Mac as well as PC. *http://www.finaldraft.com.*

A Word of Caution

Because all screenwriting programs have different features and a different "feel," they can be as personal as buying a car. One person's dream program will not be another's. The best approach is to test demos yourself.

Templates and Macros

If you can't afford a full-fledged screenwriting program, the less expensive alternative is a template or set of macros that turns your regular word processing program into a script-formatting program. Check out: *http://www.dependentfilms.net/files.html.*

Where to Buy Software

Look for sales at:

- The Writer's Computer Store: from US or Canada phone 800-272-8927 toll free, from US or Canada; *writerscomputer. com*

- Starcomp *www.leonardo.net/starcomp/* (818) 609-0330.

Information on the Internet changes rapidly, so be sure to do a search for the latest URLs and information.

Exercises

1. Correct the following incorrect sluglines:
    INT. BEDROOM – JOE'S HOUSE – NIGHT
    EXT. IN MIDDLE OF FIELD – DAY
    EXT. MASTER BEDROOM IN JOE'S HOUSE – DAY

2. Open up the following action description to provide more script verticality and isolation of major images.

    Joe steps into the living room. He turns on the light. He faces a room that is a total mess. Empty beer and pop cans are everywhere. Ash trays are filled with cigarette butts. Old newspapers are strewn about. Dirty dishes and glasses are on tables and even the floor. A radio is on, tuned to a rock station. A light from the kitchen spills into the room. Joe hesitates, then steps in the direction of the kitchen.

3. Joe is at a phone booth on a street corner. Mary is at work at a café where she is a waitress. Joe calls her. This is their brief conversation:

    "Is Mary there?" "This is Mary." "I didn't recognize your voice. This is Joe." "Why are you calling me at work?" "Mary, we need to talk. I—" "I can't talk now." "Just give me a minute." "Call me at home tonight." "This is important." "Goodbye, Joe."

    And she hangs up.

    Write this in correct screenplay format.

5

Your Screenplay's Structure:
Introduction

Through the next several chapters, tree people and forest people are going to take different paths. This is not to say you can't peek at the other group's material, but henceforth I will speak directly to your method of writing and learning.

We want to structure the story behind our concept, *The First Lady is kidnapped and held for ransom by terrorists.*

Two Views of Structure

For tree people, structure is a careful, thoughtful exercise in planning, an essential tool in the writing process. Many tree people make outlines or use index cards to organize the story and to order them in a way that strengthens dramatic structure.

Forest people, on the other hand, are apt to give little or no conscious thought to structure this early. This is not to say that structure does not concern them (though many claim it doesn't) but that it appears later and often less consciously. For forest people, structure comes naturally as the grammar of storytelling—or it had better. If it doesn't, they will find themselves becoming more like tree people to give their stories dramatic order and power.

The three-act paradigm – by which we mean a story with dramatic movement and a beginning, a middle, and an end – is so essential and underlying that its organization can be found even in the scripts of people who deny using it. There are successful Hollywood writers who reject it, deny its importance, even recoil from it, yet in analyzing their scripts, we see the paradigm at work. This suggests that the paradigm is basic to storytelling in our culture. It works.

The Two Worlds of Your Story

Stories begin in the "ordinary" world of the main character and move into the "extra-ordinary" world of the story. To the protagonist, this world is extraordinary because it is new, different, and challenging. This transition from ordinary to extraordinary marks the end of the story's "beginning." (Act One, the setup) and the beginning of the "middle" of the story (Act Two, the arena for conflict). Whether you are a tree or forest person, this transition is one of the first things you should think about.

In *E. T.* Eliot's ordinary home life includes an absent father and an older brother who ignores him. The extraordinary world begins when he lures E.T. home, creating a secret world (from mom) in which he has an alien friend.

In *The Graduate*, the ordinary world is one in which Benjamin is bored and without ambition. He creates the extraordinary world by having an affair with Mrs. Robinson. Note that protagonists participate in creating their extraordinary worlds. The action they take, called the call to action, moves us into the story.

In *A Beautiful Mind*, John Nash's ordinary world is graduate school at Princeton. But he stops going to class and decides to write a controversial, original thesis creating the extraordinary world of his own isolation and eccentricity.

If dramatic structure is about organization, what is being organized? In a word, conflict. Not random conflict but a highly focused kind, centering on your main character, his or her goal, and whatever stands between character and goal. Conflict is the essence of dramatic storytelling. David Morrell, the novelist who created Rambo, describes it in his book *Lessons From a Lifetime of Writing*:

> As far as I'm concerned, in the abstract there's only *one* plot, and it goes like this: A person or group or entity (an animal or an alien, whatever) wants something. Perhaps it's to survive a blizzard, to get married, to dominate the world, or to save a child trapped in a fire, whatever. Another person or group or entity (nature, for example, or a destructive inner self) throws up every barrier imaginable to stop that goal from being achieved.

Dramatic structure is organizing the conflict in your story. Let's look at this structure from the viewpoint of tree people.

6

STRUCTURE FOR TREE PEOPLE

In the current market, filled with so much advice and so many seemingly contradictory "rules," if you are not confused you haven't been doing your homework. In 1982, after Syd Field's influential book *Screenplay: the Foundations of Screenwriting* , a cottage industry appeared catering to growing hordes of aspiring screenwriters. Many, reading about six-digit advances to first-time writers, got dollar signs in their eyes. Now every time you turn around, someone is peddling a new paradigm, better method, or greater insight into the craft of screenwriting.

If this is true, you might ask, why am I contributing yet another book? Well, I'm hoping this book can bring some order to the chaos. I also believe that the prevailing "conflicting" theories have more in common than not and that these theories, aimed largely at tree people, ignore the needs of forest people.

So let's begin with the ABCs of structure for tree people.

Beginning, Middle, End

Creative people—even tree people—rebel at rules. Yet certain notions about what makes a successful narrative go back to 350 B.C. In his *Poetics* (Book VII), Aristotle wrote:

> Now, according to our definition, Tragedy is an imitation of an action that is complete, and whole, and of a certain magnitude; for there may be a whole that is wanting in magnitude. A whole is that which has a beginning, a middle, and an end.

What Aristotle thought about Tragedy (a certain kind of Greek play) came to be applied to stories in general: that they have beginnings, middles and endings. This solidified into a recipe for storytelling, specifying what should happen in each of the three acts. What we call the three-act paradigm has become the foundation of every other paradigm in today's crowded market of screenwriting theories.

The turn-of-the-century actor George M. Cohan said it in a different way (to paraphrase): "All stories have three acts. In the first, put your hero up a tree. In the second, throw rocks at the hero. In the third, get the hero out of the tree."

Someone added that if the hero is still alive, you have comedy; if dead, tragedy.

This storytelling model is so powerful, it spills into all narrative genres. Listen to Stephen J. Cannell, one of the most successful television producers in history, quoted in Rich Whiteside's wonderful book, *The Screenwriting Life:*

> "I write stories that have a three-act structure. Act One should define the problem. At the top of Act Two you should complicate the problem. That's usually when something in the back-story hits the hero on the back of the head that makes the problem much more complicated and dangerous than it originally was. Then during Act Two, your protagonist should be moving to solve this new, more complicated problem. And, very importantly, your antagonist should be moving to try and prevent the solution of the problem."

Stories Are About People

Some movies are plot-driven, some character-driven. Which is more important?

Surprisingly, Hollywood producers seem to side with Aristotle. Their clear preference, what they call the best movies – read "commercially successful" – are plot-driven. In Book VI of the *Poetics*, Aristotle wrote, "The plot, then, is the first principle, and, as it were, the soul of a tragedy; Character holds the second place."

Hollywood's "big effects" movies are notorious for stories where characters take a back seat to big explosions, car chases, and assorted visual effects. In contrast, the European film market, and a faction of the American independent market, prefers quieter stories that depend more on our involvement with characters.

So do people only matter in European movies or to independent American producers? Absolutely not. In the most expensive, outlandish "special effects" movie, it's what happens to people not buildings or cars that keeps us involved. When characters no longer matter or when the focus (on heroes or heroines struggling over obstacles toward their goals) goes astray, we lose the spine upon which hangs our involvement.

Consider *Jumanji*. For all its wonderful effects, the story's human interest – what happens to the people—is negligible. We moviegoers are always asking, What happens next? In *Jumanji*, who cares? As a result the movie is reduced to one animal stampede after another, and once you've seen one, you've seen them all.

Another movie script with a disastrously weak story spine is *Ali*, a movie that shows Hollywood at its worst. A lot of money was spent to do things right, and the film is beautiful to look at and very well acted. Hollywood spent all this money and skimped on the most basic thing of all, a strong, clear story. Without a central focus, *Ali* is merely a string of wonderful disconnected scenes. The story's fragmented flow is strangled by history. At almost three hours, it is repetitive and boring, but as constructed, it would have been boring after two!

Good action movies—like *Raiders of the Lost Ark, Star Wars, Jurassic Park, Romancing the Stone, Lord of the Rings*—have characters we care about. We want to know what happens to them. We become personally involved in their goals. Because we care, all the obstacles they face, all their actions, matter that much more.

Today, many movies get made in which people matter little. Some even make money because we all like to be entertained by dazzling special effects. But the movies that endure, that get rented again and again on video, regardless of genre, are movies that touch us on a personal level. Their stories are about people we care about.

Characterization is the art of creating people we care about.

Goal + Obstacle = Conflict

The Hollywood movie has evolved into a story about a hero. This meshes nicely with Hollywood being star-driven. A movie star plays a hero, and there you have it.

But not quite.

"Hero" in this sense means "main character" or protagonist (not necessarily Hercules or Robin Hood). Every movie has one—almost. There are "ensemble movies" in which many characters seem to share the spotlight – *The Breakfast Club*, for example. Upon analysis, however, they usually have a central character whose concerns or goals drive the story.

The hero or heroine is your story's main character, and s/he must want something. There must also be some obstacle that keeps them from reaching their goal. Most often this is a person, the villain or antagonist.

The easier the movie is to understand, the clearer the antagonist. In Hollywood action movies, it's usually a matter of good guy v. bad guy. There's never a doubt about who is who. In more subtle character-driven movies, the kind independents do so well, the antagonist may be "fuzzier," harder to nail down. The antagonist may have a shifting face, or even be a "negative" aspect of the protagonist.

In *Citizen Ruth* the antagonist is embodied in both sides of the abortion issue. The antagonist is politics itself, or the kind of politics that becomes blinded by its own causes. In *Chasing Amy*, although the hero's best friend opposes his affection for a lesbian, it is the hero's own immaturity that keeps him from finding "true love."

But the familiar pattern – hero or heroine with goal, antagonist in the way—means conflict, and conflict is the basis of drama. What screenplay structure does is order conflict into a beginning, middle and ending so it maximizes your story's power.

The 3-Act Paradigm

The most explicit "hard line" exposition of the three-act paradigm in the screenwriting context was made by Syd Field. My "take" on Field's Paradigm looks something like this:

ACT I	ACT II	ACT III
"put your hero up a tree"	"throw rocks"	"get hero out of the tree"
set up story	conflict	climax & resolution
Ordinary world	**Extraordinary world**	
hook, complication,	more conflict	
call to action	possible new goal	
PLOT PT	**MID PT**	
(pp20-30)	(pp45-60)	
	low point	
	PLOT PT	
	(pp75-100)	

I am more flexible than Field on the "page location" of the three major plot points. This isn't a hard science.

On the other hand, this paradigm is a foundation for screenwriting that not only works in the writing process, but also is a superb tool with which to analyze screenplays.

In Appendix 1 there are examples of this in action from 1940 to the present. In Appendix 2 is a 3-Act Paradigm Work Sheet, a useful tool when you create the dramatic structure of your own story.

My 3-Act Conversion

I'll never forget the moment I became a "true believer." I had recently finished Syd Field's book. Quasi-forest person that I am, I looked at his paradigm chart with disbelief and dismay. I decided to prove Field wrong where it counted, in the movie theater.

I went to a double bill carrying a stopwatch to monitor Field's celebrated "plot points," confident I would prove his theory wrong. The movies, *An Officer and a Gentleman* and *Harold and Maude,* couldn't possibly have anything in common. Could they?

To make a long story short, Syd Field's paradigm worked like a charm. I came out dazed—and a convert. Don't take my word for it. Rent some videos and look for the major plot points at the end of Act One, at midpoint, and at the end of Act Two. They will be there.

In Appendix 1 I've broken down dozens of very different movies into their structural foundations. Rent the video, see if you can find the script on the Internet or in a bookstore, and get to work. What better way to learn screenplay structure than to study the pros.

More on 3-Act Structure

The 3-act structure has been used in creative ways that disguise it. You'll see a movie and think that beginning-middle-end storytelling is being violated until you analyze what you've seen more carefully.

Usually these stories involve ensemble casts, in which the protagonist may not be immediately clear. Yet there is one character who, through action or theme, "oversees" the movement of the story. The structural development of these stories usually embraces one of two strategies.

In movies like *Dead Poet's Society* or *Cocoon*, a group of people in the same place and circumstances tell the story. Teacher and students at a school or the residents of a retirement home interact. Within this ensemble the story is told. But the story is driven by the decisions of one of them. Within the ensemble is a protagonist, though the role may vary, a shifting protagonist if you will.

In the second strategy, the ensemble characters are not grounded in common place and time but are related by theme. Examples are movies like *Magnolia* and *Traffic*. In the latter, we have three major story threads, which physically overlap in minor ways but are thematically related in more important ways: the drug czar and his world, including his addicted daughter; a good Mexican cop and his world; and, a good American drug agent and his world. Here I would call the drug czar, played by Michael Douglas, the protagonist (this character has the thematic overview) but the story unfolds by telling these three threaded stories in a rhythm that moves between them.

Each thread in *Traffic* has its dramatic structure, and the overall story is a sequence that moves between these threads. Imagine these threads are called A, B and C and the sequence outline of each is called A1, A2 ... A10, B1 ... B10 and C1 ... C10. The story movement of the whole then becomes something like A1, B1, A2, C1, C2, B2, A3 and so on.

Beginners sometimes confuse chronology with structure. A story need not be told chronologically to have dramatic structure—consider *Nixon*. (See Appendix 1).

Dramatic structure in a film may not be clear on first viewing. Consider the unusual movie *Memento* (2000), whose repetitive, non-chronological scenes are presented as a puzzle. At first, it seems that this story has no traditional structure at all. But dramatic structure depends on the order of information presented to the audience. Once this is understood, *Memento*'s "traditional" 3-act structure becomes clear: a hook in which the protagonist "has a condition"; a complication in which this is identified as very short-term memory loss; a call to action in which we understand he is on a mission to find and kill the man who raped and murdered his wife; a first act plot point and extraordinary world of repetition and paradox, the hero worrying that someone is setting him up; a midpoint in which a woman who has been helping him is revealed to be using him; and an end of Act Two low point in which we realize the man is trapped to continue his search forever. Here the audience as well as the non-understanding protagonist has a journey. All the same, 3-act dramatic movement is in place.

The bottom line is leading the audience to ask 'what happens next?' These creative structures, rather than violating 3-act storytelling, extend its power and possibilities.

Spin-offs of the 3-Act Paradigm

In the competitive "how to write a screenplay" cottage industry, it wouldn't pay to just sit around and agree with Syd Field. Or Aristotle. How would we get any business? So different people have examined the paradigm closely, under different lenses, and came up with variations–renaming it, or occasionally even claiming their theory "proves" Field's paradigm is dead. Right. Like God, and like the king.

What people are doing is fine-tuning the basic concept of three acts—often with useful results. Since we all must ultimately find our most effective writing method, it pays to be exposed to many explanations and variations. But understand that, despite what the gurus tell you, these are theories that rise from the three-act paradigm, without which all of them would collapse.

Some of the major variations include:

- the four-act paradigm
- David Trottier's six-events paradigm
- the seven-act paradigm
- the nine-act paradigm

- the hero's journey paradigm
- the audience's fulfillment paradigm

In essence, each of these is a variation on the original concept of beginning-middle-end storytelling.

If you don't understand a particular paradigm, it's not the end of the world. All have their proponents, and they are all more alike than different. You can quibble over how many acts a screenplay *really* has—but inevitably we're still talking about beginning-middle-end storytelling.

Here tree people can learn something from forest people: don't lose the big picture by getting lost in small details.

The 3-Act Paradigm Work Sheet

I've developed a bare-bones work sheet I use for sketching the three-act structures of my screen stories. Sometimes I take a pile along on a camping trip to structure future scripts. The work sheet, which should be self-explanatory after the rest of this chapter, is in Appendix 2. Copy it for your own use.

"American Movies Are About What Happens Next"

Actor William Macy (*Fargo*) has put this axiom, from Richard Toscan's online *Playwriting Seminars*, as forcefully as anyone:

> "The only thing I want to see when I go to see a movie—
> and I'm not being facetious at all—is what happens next.
> What's the next plot point. All I want to do is be told a story,
> and it better be a good story. It better have something to
> do with my life."

He makes two important points. The movie better have something to do with my life: it better be about people. And, what happens next: the story better have movement that keeps me guessing and interested.

No matter what paradigm speaks to you, even if none do—if you can write a movie story that puts the audience on the edge of its seat, asking, "What happens next?" you've written "a page turner" you can be proud of.

Screenwriting's cardinal sin is *to be boring*. I am going to do everything in my power to make sure you are never boring.

The Bottom Line: Finding Your Structure

Enough theory. How do you actually find your story's structure?

Let's return to: *The First Lady is kidnapped by terrorists and held for ransom.*

How do we structure this into a screenplay? First we decide on our main character. Let's say the First Lady. What does she want? A divorce.

So far, so good. We have an interesting idea—the First Lady in a bad marriage, wanting a divorce. Then she is kidnapped and held for ransom.

Let's use our work sheet to develop our structure. Working this out, we see there are many ways to develop this material. You may have better ideas than I do.

THE HOOK

Two strange characters are tailing the First Lady as she tours a children's hospital, a retirement home, and attends a library dedication.

THE COMPLICATION

At the same time, the President is having a rendezvous with his lover.

THE HERO'S CALL TO ACTION

At the end of her busy day, the First Lady meets with her lawyer. She knows her husband is having an affair and wants a divorce—political consequences be damned. Against her lawyer's advice, she decides to file.

FIRST ACT PLOT POINT

The next day, on another busy schedule, the same two people from the hook kidnap the First Lady. They are terrorists demanding that the U.S. stop supporting their enemies.

HERO'S GOAL

The First Lady fears for her safety and wants nothing more than to get out of this alive.

MIDPOINT PLOT POINT

The terrorists are kind. For the first time, the First Lady understands the political position of the foreigners, who do not get good press in the U.S. She is also falling in love with one of her kidnappers. She wants to help them.

ACT TWO PLOT POINT

The President locates where his wife is being held captive—and decides that losing his wife in an armed raid would not be an altogether bad thing. A huge Army surrounds the terrorists and First Lady. They look doomed.

HERO'S GOAL

The First Lady is now in love with one of the terrorists and does not want to leave him. She wants to negotiate a peaceful settlement.

CLIMAX & RESOLUTION

The President convinces everyone that the First Lady's offer is a ploy orchestrated by the terrorists. During the ensuing raid, the First Lady's terrorist-lover manages to save her but is killed along with all the terrorists. The First Lady, instead of being thankful for her rescue, publicly condemns her husband's overkill and announces her divorce, ruining his career.

From Logline to 3-Act Structure

Let's look at another example, using a logline from one of my students. The first task of a tree person is to move from logline to 3-act dramatic structure.

LOGLINE: A wife's marriage is jeopardized when her high school boyfriend returns home full of regrets, romance, and promises.

The Two Pillars of Structure

What's the first step in creating structure for a story? I suggest finding the 3-act paradigm's two great pillars: the transition plot points between acts one and two and between acts two and three. These dramatic moments are especially well defined.

The transition from Act Two to Three, the Second Act plot point, is the low point in the arc of the protagonist. As the main character, the wife's low point could be the apparent collapse of her marriage. Let's have the husband discover her "affair" with her ex-boyfriend and move out. Let's increase the stakes by having him take their children.

The transition from Act One to Two, the Act One plot point, is where the protagonist leaves her ordinary world, a weary routine marriage that makes her particularly vulnerable. Her extraordinary world presents romantic possibilities, a fantasy affair with her ex-boyfriend. Her life acquires new meaning, albeit one that could lead to disaster.

Let's move backwards in Act One. The call to action? When she agrees to see the ex-boyfriend. The complication? His arrival back in town. The hook? As this is a story about a marriage that might have died of neglect had not the ex-boyfriend appeared, let's start with a marital argument. We'll make it trivial, really stupid, first to show that the marriage is strong at root; second, to show how petty the couple has become in their daily routines.

If we want a happy ending, what is Act Three? The wife saves the marriage. She realizes she really loves her husband and children. To make this more solid, let's make sure she does NOT have an affair with the ex-boyfriend. We need the husband to mistakenly believe his wife has cheated on him. We can do it by having the wife meet her ex at a motel but not go through with it. She is seen, however, and the rumor reaches her husband.

The midpoint plot point? This is usually a new goal for the protagonist. In this story, the wife agrees to meet the ex in a romantic setting, giving in to his pursuit. She begins paying attention to her looks, feeling sexy again, embracing the romance the ex is bringing into her life.

So I suggest beginning with the two major plot points and then filling in the rest. Here's what the logline's structure finally looks like:

HOOK: Wife and husband argue over something silly. Their marriage is in a rut.

COMPLICATION: Wife learns her ex-boyfriend from high school is back in town. Let's say she was a cheerleader, he the football star who went off to college, got involved with someone else, and broke her heart.

CALL TO ACTION: The ex wants to see her. She agrees. They have lunch.

ACT ONE PLOT POINT: It's not merely a visit, the ex has moved back to town. He expresses regret about breaking up with her. He wants her back. Her world has changed.

MIDPOINT: She gives in to the romantic overtures of the ex, starts seeing him on the sly. Later she'll agree to meet him at a motel, to sleep with him.

ACT TWO PLOT POINT: She can't go through with sleeping with him, but they are seen together at the motel. The news gets back to the husband, who moves out with their kids.

RESOLUTION: The wife learns how important her husband and family are to her. She confronts the ex and gets him to go with her to see the husband. The ex tells the husband the truth. She and her husband reunite with a new appreciation and new passion.

Beginners are typically too verbose when they fill out the paradigm worksheet. Notice how efficiently and clearly I express each story point. When dealing with structural issues, too much language interferes with clarity. Always express yourself as efficiently and clearly as possible. As in so much of screenwriting, less is more.

Getting Ready to Write

The development above is what a tree person does before beginning to write a screenplay. Many go from the work sheet, or something similar, to a second step: writing a sequence outline. A sequence outline lists the dozen or so broad movements of your story (see the example below).

After a sequence outline, many "tree" screenwriters develop a step outline, which breaks the sequences into their individual scenes. Some writers describe each scene in one or two sentences on an individual index card, making them portable and easy to rearrange.

After the step outline, other tree people might proceed to a third step, writing a treatment. A treatment is a prose version, using almost no dialogue, written in the present tense.

Our treatment might begin: "The First Lady is making the rounds at a children's hospital. She moves from bed to bed, taking time to meet personally with the children. Outside the hospital, two suspicious characters watch her through binoculars, catching as much of her movement through the windows as possible."

I personally never write a treatment (unless a producer requires one in a for-hire deal). I do use work sheets and index cards, though not for every screenplay. I find some stories come in a great rush, demanding to be written quickly. Others simmer, taking more time to develop.

But these are your tools: the paradigm work sheet, sequence outline, step outline, and treatment. If you are a tree person you want to understand as much of your story as possible before beginning to write.

Your Project's Structure

Now it's time for you to write.

Fill out the paradigm work sheet for your script concept.

Then, if you are so inclined, write a step outline for your script (you may want to begin with the sequence outline, noting your story's dozen or so main thematic beats). If you are really a tree person, you may want to write a treatment.

The following sequence outline and step outline describe *E.T.*

Example of Sequence Outline: *E.T.*

1. "ET is stranded." (steps 1-2)
2. "Eliot is lonely." (steps 3-5)
3. "Eliot finds ET." (steps 6-11)
4. "Eliot gets to know ET." (steps 12-14)
5. "Eliot shares ET with his brother and sister." (steps 15-18)
6. "Eliot realizes that men are looking for ET." (steps 19-22)
7. "Eliot and ET are physically, spiritually connected." (steps 23-26)
8. "ET wants to go home and Eliot will help him." (steps 27-33)
9. "Men take over the house." (steps 34-36)
10. "ET is missing." (steps 37-42)
11. "ET is captured by the men." (steps 43-50)
12. "Eliot helps ET escape and catch his ride home." (steps 51-53)

Example of Step Outline: *E.T.*

1. A spacecraft has landed. Aliens collect plant samples (hook).
2. Humans arrive, scaring them off. ET is stranded (complication).
3. Eliot is ostracized and ignored by his older brother and his friends.
4. Going out to get a pizza delivery, Eliot hears a strange noise. When he throws a ball, someone or something throws it back.
5. Nobody believes him, but the older boys go out to investigate. They find tracks they assume to be a coyote's.

6. Early a.m., Eliot hears noises again. He investigates and finds ET. Both are scared stiff and run.
7. Eliot tries to bait ET back to the house (call to action).
8. Eliot defends seeing ET to mother, brother, sister. Nobody believes him.
9. Eliot waits for ET at night - and the alien comes. They meet.
10. Eliot coaxes ET into the house. They get to know one another.
11. Men from above are out searching for ET.
12. Eliot fakes illness to stay home from school and be with E.T.
13. Eliot spends day with ET, shares his toys. They get closer.
14. Later Eliot gives ET a meal.
15. After school, Eliot shows ET to his brother. His sister comes in and meets the alien.
16. Mother walks in, ET hidden, but she suspects something. Eliot says he's keeping him, only us kids can know (end of act one, plot point).
17. Men continue search for ET.
18. Eliot shows ET a map. ET gestures he is from outer space, performs magical feats.
19. Eliot sees men near the house.
20. ET brings dead flowers to life.
21. At bus stop, kids tease Eliot about his "goblin."
22. Mother hears noise upstairs, investigates. ET hidden with stuffed animals.
23. At school, Eliot's class is dissecting frogs.
24. At home alone, ET gets drunk.
25. Eliot at school also gets drunk - he and ET have magical biological connection. Eliot sets free all the frogs.
26. Mother gets call from school about Eliot. ET is with sister in kitchen but mother keeps missing him. Sister teaches ET to talk.
27. Sister shows Eliot that ET can talk. ET says, "ET phone home" - he wants to go home (midpoint).
28. Men looking for ET come in vans to house. They are bugging the kids.
29. Eliot and brother prepare to get material so ET can make a phone. Brother says ET doesn't look too hot.
30. They sneak the material into the house for ET.
31. ET builds a communication device.
32. On Halloween, the kids sneak out ET, dressed as a ghost.
33. They go to ridge to set up device, their bike magically flying.
34. When mother leaves the house on Halloween, men enter.

35. The device works and starts sending signals.
36. The house is searched and tested by the men.
37. At the ridge, Eliot begs ET not to go home.
38. Eliot falls asleep, wakes next morning at the ridge - but ET is gone.
39. Mother reports Eliot is missing. But he returns as she is being questioned, with news that ET is missing.
40. Brother takes off to look for ET, gets followed by men in car, ditches them.
41. He finds ET under an overpass, dying. A helicopter looms overhead.
42. Brother brings ET home, finally shows him to mother. Eliot believes he and ET are dying.
43. The house is invaded by men in high tech suits, house quarantined.
44. Eliot and ET are captured in adjacent beds, heavily monitored. ET is dying
45. Eliot tells sympathetic scientist that ET needs to go home in order to survive.
46. ET has no pulse. (end of act two, plot point).
47. ET left for dead, men pack up to go.
48. Eliot gets moment with ET's body.
49. When Eliot says, "I love you," ET revives.
50. ET tells Eliot his people are coming, "ET go home."
51. Eliot tells his brother that ET is alive. They kidnap ET, the brother driving the ambulance.
52. Long chase to get ET safely to the ridge in time to go home.
53. They ditch the men and make it to the ridge. ET goes home.

Exercises

1. Identify the "ordinary world" of the protagonist and the "extraordinary world" of the story in the next five movies you see. Make a habit of analyzing movies this way.
2. Take your 3-act paradigm worksheet and change the protagonist. How does this change the story's dramatic structure?
3. Rent and watch *E.T.* with the above sequence and step outlines in hand. Follow how the story develops step-by-step, sequence-by-sequence.

7

STRUCTURE FOR FOREST PEOPLE

First Draft as Discovery

Do forest people need to worry about structure? Of course they do. But they can worry about it later in the writing process and in a different, less obsessive way.

As a forest person, once you get your concept—First Lady kidnapped by terrorists and held for ransom—you want to jump in and start writing script, making your decisions along the way.

Despite what you hear from "tree person" gurus, there's nothing wrong with your approach—if, and I repeat if, you can make it work. Your goal is "to discover" your story not using a prepared outline but as you write it.

Your initial notion of structure may be vague, no more than the certainty your story will eventually have a beginning, middle, and end. You may only know your beginning, but that may be enough. A forest person trusts in writing his or her way to the solutions.

Being a "sometimes forest person" myself (and we can treat different projects differently!), I offer a "shortcut" I call the Bare Bones Structure for Forest People.

Bare Bones Structure

If you are writing your screenplay on a computer, write it as four files. If you use a typewriter (yes, people still write on typewriters!), write your script in four different "parts" or "modules." Each of these files or modules will be 25-30 pages in length, and you will make sure of one thing:

Each file or module except the last must end with a zinger of a plot point.

See what I'm doing?

Since forest people prefer "winging it," this system allows you to wing it only one-quarter of the script at a time. Your four files will naturally become Act One, the first half of Act Two, the second half of Act Two, and Act Three.

This is all the worrying you will have to do about structure. By ending each file/module with a big twist in the story, your major plot points will fall exactly where they belong.

No muss, no fuss.

The Hero Leads the Way

By jumping right in, you invite magic into the process—the story can suddenly seem to be writing itself. Just because it's flowing, however, does not mean it's going where it should.

Forest people need to constantly remind themselves that their story is about their hero or heroine. The main character needs to lead the way, occupy center stage, and focus the story. That character's goal or journey is the script's dramatic spine.

Check yourself. Be alert to scenes where your hero is absent. Too many? You're in trouble. After five pages without an appearance, I'd begin to worry. Personally, I get nervous after two.

The hero leads the way. Memorize it.

The Villain Must Be Formidable

The other character you must attend to is your "villain" or antagonist, the person (or force) who stands between your hero and his or her goal. Most antagonists written by beginners are cream puffs.

The meaner, tougher, and cleverer the antagonist, the more "rocks" s/he throws at the hero. The greater the hero's jeopardy, the more the hero struggles against the antagonist, and the greater the conflict and drama.

This is no easy accomplishment, particularly in genres where the stereotypical monster-villain, which is common in action-adventure movies, is out of place.

For example, consider *The Graduate*. Benjamin, the hero, initially has an affair with Mrs. Robinson. Later he discovers he is attracted to Elaine, Mrs. Robinson's daughter (the lover/mother has forbidden him to see her), and a new goal, the "true goal," kicks into motion. First Mrs. Robinson, then Elaine, and later Mr. Robinson become obstacles to Benjamin's winning Elaine's heart.

Sometimes, the antagonist can be a "family" of characters, literally or metaphorically, rather than an obvious individual. *The Graduate*'s antagonist is the Robinson family. What makes this "villain" formidable is its growing opposition. First, Mrs. Robinson bans Benjamin from seeing Elaine when he isn't even interested in her. When he is interested in her, Elaine herself won't see him after he admits to an affair with her mother. Finally Mr. Robinson confronts him after learning of the affair. Each representation of "the Robinson villain" is more menacing than its predecessor.

"American Movies Are About What Happens Next"

What propels *The Graduate* is not the "paradigm-perfect" hero-villain confrontation of most movies but its suspense. We want to know what happens next. The antagonist keeps shifting between different representations until it becomes a social force, the middle-class values Benjamin is bored with, the forces that make him want a "different" summer, his initial goal.

What tree people can learn from this is to trust the story over the paradigm. This does not mean the beginning-middle-end storytelling paradigm doesn't "work," but that it is a flexible tool for planning and analyzing.

I cannot over-emphasize this: the 3-act structure is not a formula but a set of guidelines. It is the storytelling grammar of our culture. A perfectly structured story without interesting characters, without twists and surprises beyond its "necessary" plot points, without human and universal themes, is lifeless.

I can imagine how a tree person might "over-work" the spine of *The Graduate*, clarifying the protagonist-antagonist (hero-villain) conflict but also making the story more ordinary in the process.

But like the blueprint for a house, you need structure. You begin with it. But you don't live in it! You structure your story to guide the script. Along the way, things may change. You need to trust your story, to let the heart direct the head –without decapitating yourself! In this comedy, it doesn't matter if the villain is a family that takes turns standing in Benjamin's way. His goal is always clear, and the obstacles present unexpected twists and increasing danger to Benjamin's winning Elaine.

Exercises

1. Rent a movie in your story's genre. As you watch it keep track of how much consecutive time the hero is absent. What does this tell you about focus on the hero?
2. List memorable antagonists from movies you've seen. What makes them memorable?
3. Look for Bare Bones Structure in movies: the first act plot point, that transition from ordinary to extraordinary worlds; the major midpoint twist that sometimes redefines the protagonist's goal; the second act plot point, the protagonist's low point. The more you can identify this structure, the more natural it will feel, and the more naturally you will use it to organize your own stories.

8

Basic Skills

Whether tree person or forest person, screenwriters must master certain basic skills. It takes writers, particularly fiction writers, a while to learn screenwriting's crisp, clean, focused storytelling. In this sense, screenwriting is a bit like poetry. Stacy Coffey, a former student of mine, put it this way:

> Like poetry, in screenwriting you are trying to show something with words, often with as few words as possible. While some poetry is wordy, many poems are more of a distillation of an idea or feeling. Really, that's screenwriting. A script distills a story down to its absolute essence. Everything not necessary must be boiled away, or chopped out with a gas-powered chain saw, an image that's more appealing to my iconoclastic nature.

In screenwriting, "less is more." Put another way (the Johnny Cochran School of Screenwriting), "When it doubt, leave it out!"

The challenge in screenwriting is to write in an entertaining way while still respecting the form's incredible economy. A good example of minimalist writing with an entertaining style is the opening of Max Adams' screenplay *Excess Baggage*. (This script got butchered in development and rewrites; this is from her original script).

Example of *Excess Baggage*

```
FADE IN: EXT. PORTLAND, OREGON
(ESTABLISHING)—DAY

Portland, home of rivers, bridges, and
more parks than you can shake a stick at.
The Columbia River, spanned by the Highway
5 and 205 bridges, glistens a muddy brown
in the sunlight; the Willamette glitters
off to the south.
```

INT. PARKING GARAGE/UPPER LEVEL—DAY

EMILY ROSE T. HOPE cut her teeth on a million dollar teething ring, and it was bitter—too bitter. It left her an old woman's attitude in a young woman's body.

She idly taps a cellular phone's keypad with one perfectly manicured nail as she stares through the parking level's open struts at a distant bridge—and an approaching river barge.

The barge draws closer to the bridge. Closer. Closer still.

She takes a drag off a cigarette, stubs it out, and dials a number on the phone's keypad.

EXT. BRIDGE—DAY

AMADEUS T. HOPE, an older man who most assuredly broke his teeth on a Rolls Royce, stands in a phone booth just off the bridge, waiting for the phone to ring and caressing a briefcase like it contained a million dollars—which it does.

Nearby, idle joggers in the park are more than obviously undercover cops.

The phone rings and Amadeus lifts it.

> AMADEUS
>
> I'm here.
>
> EMILY (FILTERED)
>
> Amadeus T. Hope?
>
> AMADEUS
>
> Yes.
>
> EMILY (FILTERED)
>
> Did you bring the money?
>
> AMADEUS
>
> Yes.
>
> EMILY (FILTERED)
>
> Listen carefully.

This is clean, crisp screenwriting.

Example of good screenwriting

Most beginning screenwriters overwrite: too much description, too much dialogue, too much choreography of the actors' movements.

Here's a sample of crisp, clean screenwriting from one of my online students, Averil Meehan from Ireland. Notice how clear the focus is, and how direct and simple the writing is.

```
EXT. STREET—DAY

A lorry stops at a traffic light.

MEGAN, a rather bedraggled fifteen year
old, pulls back the cover. She grabs her
plastic bag of belongings and jumps off.

Megan looks round, then runs to a shop
doorway. Megan watches the lorry drive
off, looks up and down the street, then
edges out on to the pavement.

She walks down the street gazing about
her, and gives a little skip. She walks on
swinging her plastic bag.

EXT. STREET—CHIP SHOP—NIGHT

It is raining.

Megan is walking slowly, dragging her bag.
She stops at a chip shop. She goes inside.

INT. CHIP SHOP—NIGHT

Megan looks at the price list. She takes a
few coins out of her pocket, counts them
then goes to the counter.

PAUL, a thirty year old, is behind it.
SYLVIE, his pregnant wife, is setting
tables in the sit-in area.

                    MEGAN
          Half a bag of chips.

                    PAUL
          We don't do half bags.

Megan sets her coins on the counter.

                    MEGAN
          Whatever I can get for that.

                    PAUL
          You deaf or what?
```

> MEGAN
>
> Please. I'm hungry.
>
> PAUL
>
> I feed you, I'll have half the
> bleedin' city in here.
>
> Go on, clear out!

Megan stares at him.

Paul races round the end of the counter,
his fist raised.

Megan runs out.

EXT. STREET—CHIP SHOP—NIGHT

Megan stands outside and stares through
the window. A group of men come out. She
holds back against the wall and watches
them eat.

A woman comes out carrying a steaming
parcel. Megan approaches her.

> MEGAN
>
> Can I have a few chips?

The woman stares at her.

> MEGAN
>
> Please. I'm hungry.

The woman sniffs in disgust, then turns
and walks away.

Paul runs out.

> PAUL
>
> I warned you, clear off!

Megan runs down the street.

EXT. STREET—SHOP DOORWAY—NIGHT—LATER

It is still raining. Megan is sheltering
in a shop doorway, lying wrapped in a
cardboard box, shivering.

She watches the chip shop on up the
street.

A man comes out, stands a few feet from
her, eating from his bag.

A bus comes along. He flings the bag on the
ground and gets on the bus.

```
Megan dashes over to the bag, takes it
back to her cardboard shelter and starts
to eat hungrily.
```

Notice the strong verbs: edges out, races, holds back, counts, stares, sniffs, flings. Action verbs are a screenwriter's best weaponry.

Example of poor screenwriting

In contrast, consider this:

```
INT. LARGE SITTING ROOM IN A MANSION IN
ENGLAND—DAY

WE HEAR CLASSICAL MUSIC being PLAYED on
a PIANO. WE SEE a PAINTING on a wall of
a little blond girl holding a doll and
sitting on a gold chair. WE SEE VARIOUS
ART OBJECTS on tables and SEVERAL CANES
against the wall. Next to a FIREPLACE
leans a very exquisite DIAMOND-STUDDED and
RUBY WALKING STICK. At the opposite end of
the room is a HIGH-BACK LEATHER CHAIR next
to a SMALL TABLE.

A very thin, distinguished gray-haired
servant named NIGEL ENTERS CARRYING A TRAY
with a TEAPOT, CUP AND SAUCER, PITCHER,
and SEVERAL PINE CONES on it with a
NEWSPAPER UNDER HIS ARM. He walks over to
the piano.
```

There are many things wrong here:

- Capital letters are overused and distracting; use them sparingly. You must capitalize a character name the first time but after that, avoid caps. SOUNDS used to be capitalized but this has dropped out of fashion.
- "We" smacks of directing the movie.
- The descriptions are overwritten, novelistic.
- Too much detail in the slugline. Put it in the action element.

I would rewrite this as follows:

```
INT. ENGLISH MANSION—SITTING ROOM—DAY

The room is large, expensively decorated,
with a fireplace.
```

> Someone is playing classical music on a
> piano.
> NIGEL, a servant, enters with a tray for
> teatime. He marches to the piano.

See the difference? In fiction, rhetoric sets the scene—in a movie, the camera will set the scene. The writer's job is to tell the story, simply. The writer is not the set designer. "Expensively decorated, with a fireplace" is all that is needed. If certain objects, like the walking stick, have dramatic importance, mention them. Otherwise only present essentials.

Here is another example that reads like fiction writing. I've rewritten it below.

> EXT. KNASH HOUSE—OUTSIDE - DAY
>
> The house is huge, made sometime in the
> 40's or 50's and shows its age, the paint
> is flaking off, the roof needs some repair,
> and a few of the windows are cracked.
>
> The house sits on a 1-2 acre lot, within a
> small town neighborhood, but looks like it
> should be out in the country somewhere.
>
> Around the house are rows of old cars.
> Most of the cars are 60's to early 70's
> muscle cars, in various stages of being
> restored or needing to be restored.
>
> Behind the house, wherever there aren't
> any cars or car parts, there are animal
> pens set up, housing various sorts of
> animals—a couple of colts in one, maybe
> an emu or kangaroo in another, rabbits, a
> donkey, and some various animals. A few
> big dogs are running loose, and chickens
> and a few other birds are loose, roaming
> around the yard.
>
> A rather beat-up four-wheel drive pickup
> pulls up to the side of the house. CALI,
> 30s, pretty, wearing a blackjack dealer
> uniform and firmly grasping a newspaper,
> steps down out of the truck. A couple
> dogs run to meet her. Cali greets them
> and rushes down a row of cars across the
> front of the house, sidestepping chickens
> here and there. As she passes one car that

```
is jacked up, Cali doesn't notice there
are two sets of legs sticking out from
underneath it.
FREDDY, 40s, good looking, and MICKEY, 12,
long-blonde hair that is always a little
messy, are working under the car trying to
pull a transmission.
Cali enters the house.
```

This is *HUGELY* overwritten fiction writing. Here is screenwriting:

```
EXT. NASH HOUSE—DAY
The huge house shows its age. It sits on a
large lot.
Around the house are old cars in various
stages of restoration.
Behind the house, animal pens crowd among
the cars. A zoo: colts, rabbits, donkeys,
a kangaroo. Dogs and chickens roam loose.
A beat-up pickup pulls to the side of the
house.
Getting out is CALI, 30s, wearing her
blackjack dealer's uniform. On her way to
the house she passes a car out of which
stick two pairs of legs. Mechanics at
work.
Cali enters the house.
```

See the difference? In screenwriting, less is more.

Here are other "basic skills" of the craft of screenwriting.

Character Descriptions

The first time a character is introduced, s/he is described. Almost without exception, beginning screenwriters "over-describe" the character.

Let me show you a variety of character introductions:

- CITIZEN RUTH: "She is around 30." That's it!
- BIG NIGHT: "PRIMO, the chef, is at the stove. Brooding, intense, he is in his late 30s but seems older than his years." "His younger brother, SECONDO—early 30s, handsome, charming but high strung."
- LONE STAR: "We see SAM DEEDS, the sheriff, driving. Sam is 40, quietly competent to the point of seeming moody." In

a spec script, avoid writing "we see" or "we hear." It's always redundant, hence fat.

- TO DIE FOR: "Suzanne, 26 years old. Her blonde hair is pulled back and tied with a black bow."
- GET SHORTY: "CHILI PALMER, late 30s, sits in a booth with TOMMY CARLO, a low-level mob type."
- QUIZ SHOW: "The hand belongs to DICK GOODWIN, late 20s."
- THE BIG LEBOWSKI: "...a fortyish man in Bermuda shorts and sunglasses at the dairy case. He is the Dude. His rumpled look and relaxed manner suggest a man in whom casualness runs deep."
- SILENCE OF THE LAMBS: "CLARICE STARLING ... Trim, very pretty, mid-20s." "DR. HANNIBAL LECTER ... A face so long out of the sun, it seems almost leached—except for the glittering eyes, and the wet red mouth."
- BULL DURHAM: "ANNIE SAVOY, mid 30's, touches up her face. Very pretty, knowing, outwardly confident. Words flow from her Southern lips with ease, but her view of the world crosses Southern, National and International borders. She's cosmic."

You have some leeway here, as the last two examples suggest, but note that one of your options is not to write like a novelist or short story writer, providing detailed descriptions of the character. "Around 30" often is quite enough!

According to screenwriting lore, there's a reason for brevity in character description. Consider something like "JOE is 25 and stands five-foot-two-and-half-inches in his bare feet. His black hair is parted in the middle and glistens from too much hair cream. He has a dimple in his chin which, when he smiles, is embraced by dimples on each cheek. His nose is too small for his face."

A producer reads it and thinks, "My God! I could never find an actor meeting that description!" And he passes.

Give the producer "around 30." He can handle that.

Descriptions of Place

The same economy applies to describing places. All you need are a few well-chosen details, economically expressed.

Here are some samples that describe place:

- *Citizen Ruth:* "The hallway is carpetless, and the paint on the walls stained and chipped."
- *Dead Man Walking:* "As she walks we see snatches of the neighborhood. It has seen better days, but there is a warmth here, a sense of community."
- *A Fish Called Wanda:* "On a bed in a Japanese-style basement room..."
- *Sling Blade:* "It's an all-American girl's room. Everything is pink. There are stuffed animals everywhere and posters of pop idols."
- *The Ice Storm:* "A large New England Colonial, with a few modern additions and touches."
- *Chasing Amy:* "It's a rented loft place with high ceilings, wood floors, and sparse furnishings..."
- *Good Will Hunting:* "The bar is dirty, more than a little run down."

Characterization

Describing a character is one thing; bringing that character to life quite another. Characters need to be "unforgettable." Physical, emotional, and verbal behavior all contribute to personality and character.

Here are some tips:

- Establish your hero's character early, even before the call to action. Show us short visual scenes that tell us something. Imagine your hero or heroine on the golf course swinging at the ball, driving for the green, watching the flight of the ball. And then:

  o pounding the club against the grass.

  o staring silently across the green, fuming.

  o grinning, shaking his or her head and slapping the side of it.

See what three different characters we've suggested?

- Reveal as much as possible through action, not dialogue.
- Put characters in conflict so we learn about them from their reactions.
- Give characters choices so we learn their likes and dislikes.

- Give characters a history or "back story," things that happened to them in the past that boil into the present tense of the story.
- Give characters unusual hobbies, idiosyncratic personal habits, pet phrases, and other things that distinguish them.
- Make your characters believable, yet larger than life. Make us admire your hero and cringe at your antagonist. Give them contrary characteristics, a weakness in your hero, something we admire in your antagonist.
- Show us how other people react to them, what they say about them.

Good actors can create "character" even from bad scripts—but don't use their skill as a crutch. Better to write strong characterizations even poor actors can get across.

Action Scenes

Do not overwrite action scenes. As a collaborator, it is not your business to direct the actors or choreograph scenes in great detail. Break action into small paragraphs—no more than five lines each—with a blank space between them.

Shane Black (*Lethal Weapon*) has been particularly successful in creating a flow of action driven by white space (from *American Screenwriters*):

> "I've seen scripts where the first page looks like huge blocks of paragraphic text, which no one's even going to read. But on my favorite pages, the action is continuous and has a lot of short slug lines. The attention goes down rather than across. It flows, it reads as if you're following the action."

The conclusion to my *Creative Screenwriting* article, "The Rhetoric of Action":

> ...the writer must describe action with economy and imagery, bringing the scene to life on the page. For this goal, verbs are the heavy-hitters and simple sentence patterns, rhythmically broken up with compound or modifying elements, build the foundation of the narrative structure.

...Always remember you are writing for the SCREEN:

S implify!
C reate
R eadable
E fficient
E vocative
N arration"

Simplify! Create readable efficient evocative narration in your action scenes.

Examples of Action Scenes

Here are some examples of action writing from contemporary screenplays.

From *Shakespeare in Love* by Marc Norman and Tom Stoppard, a sword-fight:

```
...the fight has started.

Wessex slashes at Will. Will knows how to
fight. He parries and thrusts. Wessex is
surprised. The fight goes fast and furious
around the stage, until Will thrusts
accurately at Wessex's chest ... and would
have killed him but for the button on his
sword-point.

Wessex grapples with him, and now it
becomes a parody of the Hamlet duel.
Wessex's unbuttoned sword falls to the
ground. Will puts his foot on it, tosses
Wessex his own safe sword, picks up
Wessex's sword and continues to fight until
he has Wessex at his mercy.
```

Notice there is not a single dependent clause in this writing; it is all simple and compound sentences.

Here's a short fight scene from *The Fight Club* by Jim Uhls:

```
Jack swings another roundhouse that slams
right under Tyler's ear. The sound, soft and
flat. Tyler punches Jack in the stomach. The
Guys move closer, cheering the fight. Tyler
and Jack move clumsily, throwing punches.
They breathe heavier, their eyes red and
bright. They drool saliva and blood. They
each hurt badly and become dizzier from
every impact. [script from Internet]
```

Another example from *Smoke Signals* by Sherman Alexie:

```
As he walks toward the game, Thomas is
transporting, in an assembly line fashion,
a plastic chair, a small end table, and a
portable radio.
```

> He has all three items set in a line: the radio in front, then the end table, and the chair at the rear.
>
> Thomas picks up the last item in line, the chair, walks it to the front and sets it down.
>
> Then he walks to the back of the line and picks up the end table, walks to the front of the line, and sets it in front of the chair.
>
> Then he walks to the back of the line, picks up the radio, and then walks to the front of the line again and sets it down in front of the end table.
>
> He repeats this process again and again, making sure, steady, and slightly crazy progress toward the court.

This rhetoric is a bit more sophisticated than our previous example, but notice how Alexie breaks the action into single-line paragraphs, an "airy" strategy he continues through the entire screenplay.

An example from Alan Ball's *American Beauty:*

> Lester's REMOTE-CONTROLLED MODEL JEEP is zooming across the floor of the family room, expertly maneuvering corners and narrowly avoiding crashing.
>
> Lester is sprawled on the couch in his underwear, drinking a BEER and controlling the car. His working out is beginning to produce results. The room, too, seems changed: sloppier, more lived in.
>
> Carolyn enters through the kitchen, flushed and angry. She just stands there, staring at Lester. After a moment, he looks up at her.

Though closer to fiction rhetoric, a novelist would add considerably more detail.

These examples demonstrate the possible range within "minimalist" rhetoric. You can write detail, and should, but you need to make your script a quick, easy read.

Extended Action Scenes

The Hollywood "blockbuster" *Pearl Harbor*, despite its sappy love and buddy stories, excels in its action scenes. Here is how Randall Wallace set up the attack in an early draft.

```
EXT. PEARL HARBOR—DAY

The harbor lies quiet. It's a sleepy
Sunday morning.

Children are playing, officers are stepping
from their houses in their shorts to get
the morning paper...

EXT. MOUNTAINSIDE—OAHU—DAY

Hawaiian Boy Scouts are hiking on a side
of one of the mountains overlooking Pearl.

Suddenly booming over the mountain, barely
ten feet above the summit, comes a stream
of planes. The boys are awed. What is this?

EXT. PEARL HARBOR—DAY

QUICK INTERCUTS –

Between the approach of the Japanese
planes, and sleepy Pearl Harbor...

–The planes, in formation, their
propellers spinning, their engines
throbbing...

–Pearl Harbor, with the ships silent,
their engines cold, their anchors steady
on the harbor bottom.

–The Japanese submarines heading in.

–The American destroyers docking, instead
of going out to search for them.

–Another formation of Japanese bombers
climbing high, into attack position.

–The Japanese torpedo planes dropping down
to the level of the ocean, their engines
beginning to scream.

–The American planes bunched on the
airfields.

ON THE JAPANESE CARRIERS, Yamamoto and his
staff huddle tensely, over their battle
maps.
```

> ON THE JAPANESE CARRIER DECKS, the second
> wave of planes is being brought up and
> loaded with munitions...the Japanese flag
> snaps tautly in the wind...
>
> ON THE GOLF COURSE NEAR PEARL HARBOR,
> American officers are laughing on the
> putting green near the clubhouse, where
> the American flag droops from the flagpole,
> limply at peace.
>
> -The Japanese planes roaring down just
> over the wave tops of Pearl Harbor itself.
>
> -Children playing in the early morning
> sun, looking up as they see the planes
> flash by. The children look - they've never
> seen this many, flying this low...but they
> are not alarmed, only curious.
>
> The images come faster and faster, the
> collision of Japan's determination and
> America's innocence.

Notice how easy this is to read—the key is using the "QUICK INTERCUTS" slugline rather than individual sluglines. For long sequences of action, this is a good model.

The Screenwriter's Use of Time

A common mistake of beginning screenwriters is an incorrect use of and management of time.

Consider the following scene:

> INT. BATHROOM—NIGHT
>
> Jane comes in and draws a bath. She steps
> into the tub. She gets comfortable, closes
> her eyes and enjoys a long soak.

The rhetoric of this scene is perfectly acceptable in fiction but completely unacceptable in screenwriting. This is because in a screenplay we are describing what happens on the screen. If we take the scene above literally, here is what happens:

- Jane enters the bathroom.
- She draws a bath. How long does this take? Five minutes? The screenwriter is telling us to watch water fill a tub for five minutes!

- She gets into the tub.
- She closes her eyes and takes a long bath. How long is long? Ten minutes? Half an hour? Again, the screenwriter is telling us to sit through this!

Here is how a screenwriter would write this scene.

```
INT. BATHROOM—NIGHT

Jane comes into the bathroom. She turns on
the water to fill the tub.

INT. BATHROOM—NIGHT—LATER

Jane is stretched out in the tub, her eyes
closed.
```

See the difference? I've had students write "an hour later" in the middle of a scene, not realizing that they are telling the audience to sit watching for an hour!

Screenplay Rhetoric

Good screenplay rhetoric is simple, clean and crisp. Complex sentences are almost never used.

Here is an example of good screenplay rhetoric, from the end of John Guare's wonderful screenplay, *Atlantic City*.

```
INT. TROCADERO HOTEL—CORRIDOR—DAY

Grace, all dolled up in a mink coat and a
hat, is quite apprehensive. Grace walks
down the corridor to Room 307.

She rings the doorbell.

Alfie opens the door. The card game is
still going on in the room.

          ALFIE
     Yes? I think you have the wrong
room.

Grace holds out the last bit of cocaine in
the silver foil. Alfie's jaw drops.

          GRACE
     One thousand.

          ALFIE
     Why not?
```

```
He reaches into his pocket and hands her
a thousand dollar bill. He shuts the door.

Grace turns and walks back up the corridor
holding up the thousand-dollar bill.

Lou is standing at the other end of the
corridor. He applauds her.

She takes his arm. They leave.

EXT. BOARDWALK—DAY

Grace and Lou walk down the Boardwalk. She
proudly holds his arm.

Behind them, a wrecking ball strikes a
building, preparing to demolish it. The
building won't give.

The ball hits it again. The building won't
give.

THE END
```

Rhetorically, this is a step above "See Spot run." Variety is added with compound verbs and modifying elements but not a single subordinate clause or complex sentence!

Dialogue

Dialogue obviously comes out of character. People from different backgrounds use different vocabularies and speaking styles. If your dialogue reflects this, you will avoid another common mistake: having all characters sound alike.

Brad Mirman, screenwriter of *Knight Moves, Body of Evidence, Truth or Consequences N.M.*, has a website on which he offers advice to new writers. Here's what he has to say about dialogue:

> One of the most blatant signs of a new writer is that all the characters speak the same. They have the same vocabulary, the same cadence to their speech. This is because the writer is writing all the characters as himself. He is not looking to the dark, light, happy, sad, male, female sides of himself. He is writing all the characters as the total assembled package of himself that he presents to the world.

Mirman compares how different people might say the same thing:

- 21-YEAR-OLD MALE: Man, I squashed this cat on the way over.

- 23-YEAR-OLD FEMALE: On the way here tonight... I think I ran over a cat.
- 57-YEAR-OLD MALE: Hey, you know what? Comin' here I flattened some cat.
- 52-YEAR-OLD FEMALE: Oh, dear, I believe I may have run over some poor kitty.

Good dialogue goes somewhere; it has direction. Dialogue must move the story forward and simultaneously establish character. It also creates tension and suspense.

Good dialogue is often oblique, askew. We sense much more is being said than the literal words exchanged. This "other meaning" is called subtext. Ordinary speech is often boring, but good dialogue is crafted to add tension and mystery, direction and conflict.

A pejorative term for poor dialogue is "on the nose" dialogue, dialogue in which a character explicitly states what s/he wants or feels. There is no subtext, no secret, no mystery. But most interesting people, certainly most interesting characters, don't speak this way.

Here are some things you can do to improve your dialogue:

- Read your script aloud! The written word is not the spoken word.
- Even better, get your script into the hands of actors. Do a "staged reading." Your ear will catch what your eye missed.
- Listen to people around you on buses, in restaurants, at parties.
- Listen for idiosyncratic patterns you can borrow and adapt. However, do not make the mistake of believing that "real speech" is the goal. Dialogue is always crafted—it's more interesting than real speech but gives the illusion of real speech.
- Rewrite your dialogue and read it aloud again.

Another common mistake is weighing down dialogue with exposition, with facts we need to know to understand the story.

"This reveals the amateur writer faster than anything I know," says William Kelley, who wrote *Witness*. "Exposition is necessary. There's no question about it. But, you do it as unobtrusively as you possibly can; and as you get on through a screenplay, go back through and wherever there's exposition see if you can possibly leave it out. Or have it appear in any other way. I mean, a newspaper, an old yellowed newspaper article, or a radio broadcast or some other thing in any way you can, try to get exposition out of your dialogue." (*American Screenwriters*)

Communicating exposition is always a challenge best handled in ways that don't draw attention to it. If a character walks onto a street filled with cars from the 1930s, we know – without being told – that we are in a certain era. This is visual exposition. Poor exposition might have a character say, "I haven't been this angry since last year, in 1935!"

If you must present exposition in dialogue, make it flow naturally out of another focus of the conversation. Avoid dialogue that shouts, "Look at me! I'm exposition and here are some things you need to know!"

Think of yourself as a doctor and exposition as a pill. You want to give it to the reader or viewer without them realizing they're taking medicine.

Examples of Dialogue

Dialogue comes out of character and action: what a character says depends on who they are and what situation they are in.

Amateur dialogue tends to fall into exposition and "chit-chat," realistic and boring speech that goes nowhere and, in terms of the story, means nothing.

Gripping dialogue is usually driven by conflict, and sometimes this conflict is most important at the subtext level, the meaning "below the surface" of what is actually being said. In this scene from Nora Ephron's *When Harry Met Sally*, the literal argument is really about something deeper and masks a growing attraction between the characters. (To save space, this is written in a published screenplay format, with nothing but the essential action, so you can focus on dialogue.)

```
SALLY: What do you do with these women? Do
you just get up out of bed and leave?
HARRY: Sure.
SALLY: Well, explain to me how you do it.
What do you say?
HARRY: I say, I have an early meeting, an
early haircut, an early squash game.
SALLY: You don't play squash.
HARRY: They don't know that. They just met
me.
SALLY: That's disgusting.
HARRY: I know. I feel terrible.
SALLY: You know, I am so glad I never got
involved with you. I just would have ended
up being some woman you had to get up out
```

of bed and leave at three o'clock in the morning and go clean your andirons. And you don't even have a fireplace. Not that I would know this.

HARRY: Why are you getting so upset? This is not about you.

SALLY: Yes, it is. You're an affront to all women. And I'm a woman.

HARRY: Hey, I don't feel great about this, but I don't hear anyone complaining.

SALLY: Of course not. You're out the door too fast.

HARRY: I think they have an okay time.

SALLY: How do you know?

HARRY: What do you mean, how do I know? I know.

SALLY: Because they...?

HARRY: Yes, because they...

SALLY: How do you know they're really...

HARRY: What are you saying, they fake orgasm?

SALLY: It's possible.

HARRY: Get outta here.

SALLY: Why? Most women, at one time or another, have faked it.

HARRY: Well, they haven't faked it with me.

SALLY: How do you know?

HARRY: Because I know.

SALLY: Oh right. That's right. I forgot. You're a man.

HARRY: What's that supposed to mean?

SALLY: Nothing. It's just that all men are sure it never happens to them, and most women at one time or another have done it, so you do the math.

HARRY: You don't think I can tell the difference?

SALLY: No.

HARRY: Get outta here.

```
Harry bites into his sandwich. Sally just
stares at him. A seductive look comes onto
her face.
SALLY: Oooh!...Oh! Oooh!
HARRY: Are you okay?
Sally, her eyes closed, ruffles her hair
seductively.
SALLY: Oh, God!
Harry is beginning to figure out what Sally
is doing.
SALLY: Oooh! Oh, God!
```

And so on, to the famous punch line, "I'll have what she's having."

First, notice that the dialogue is like a tennis match. It volleys back and forth, one person scores a point, then the other. Notice that the focus shifts, so that within this one scene there are several scenes. Harry's, "Get outta here," becomes a verbal fingerprint for his character. This is great dialogue because it is engaging, humorous, and most importantly, part of the journey they are taking toward one another.

Another important question to ask in each scene is what does the character want? This is what the actor will ask (all screenwriters should take an acting class!).

In this scene from *Sling Blade* by Billy Bob Thornton, the action is driven by the actor's goal. Near the film's end, Karl has entered carrying the "sling blade" to set things right with the abusive Doyle, who is drinking beer and watching TV.

```
DOYLE: Where's ever'body else? You seen
'em? I thought I told you to get the hell
moved out of here anyway.
KARL: How does a feller go about gettin'
ahold of the police?
DOYLE: Pick up the fuckin' phone and call
'em, I guess.
KARL: What numbers do you punch?
DOYLE: I told you to get away from here,
didn't I? I'm tryin' to relax and look at
TV. What are you doin' with that piece of
iron? I swear to God you're the weirdest
son of a bitch I ever heard of.
KARL: I aim to kill you with it.
```

```
DOYLE: Yeah, okay. Well, to get the police
you push 911. You'll need to tell 'em
to send an ambulance, too. Or a hearse.
You fuckin' idiot. You're gonna kill me.
(laughs)
```

And Karl does—and immediately calls the police.

Since we, the audience, know what's on Karl's mind when he enters the room with the blade, the tension in the scene is slow and deliberate—the unsuspecting Doyle giving directions for his own murder.

Notice, too, the way "g's" are dropped ("gettin'") and the use of dialect spelling. If suitable for the character, this is a good device if not overdone. You must always remember your goal is to present an easy read. With foreign accents, it is better to state this in the action ("Joseph speaks with a German accent") rather than try to suggest it with idiosyncratic spelling, which slows down the reading.

We find an excellent example of subtext in *The Straight Story* by John Roach & Mary Sweeney. It's a very simple scene. Before Alvin begins his incredible journey, riding a lawn mower to visit his distant brother, his daughter Rose goes to the grocery store to buy him supplies. Notice how she transfers her grief and fear, not wanting her father to make the trip, to a grocery item. The scene is not about braunschweiger but her anxiety. Rose takes the items to the counter. Brenda is the checkout girl.

```
BRENDA: (a statement) Havin' a party.
ROSE: Oh ... Jeez I love parties.
BRENDA: Yah, me too.
ROSE: So where's it at?
BRENDA: Where's what at?
ROSE: Your party.
BRENDA: I'm not havin' a party. I thought
you're havin' a party.
ROSE: I am?
BRENDA: Well, yah ... look at all that
braunschweiger.
ROSE: Yah it's a lot of braunschweiger.
It's for my dad ... for his ... trip. My
dad ... He ... is going to ... Wisconsin.
BRENDA: Oh Wisconsin! A real party state.
ROSE: I hate braunschweiger.
```

The most ordinary setting—a checkout stand—can serve as the arena for revealing emotional material. Nor does it take much time when handled skillfully. Every line works, the focus is tight, and that idle chitchat doesn't dilute the scene's energy. In amateur hands, this scene could be disastrous, full of small talk that goes nowhere. Here the progression is logical, direct, concise and efficient, all moving toward the "punch line," toward the subtext: "I hate that my dad is going on this trip."

For a lesson in economy of dialogue, compare two versions of David Mamet's *American Buffalo*. As he did with *Oleanna* and *Glengary Glen Ross*, Mamet just moved the play to film, but look how the dialogue was pruned. What was cut from the film is enclosed in brackets. The dialogue sequence is cut by half:

```
BOB: Ruthie isn't mad at you.
[TEACH: She isn't?]
[BOB: No.]
TEACH: How do you know?
[BOB: I found out.]
[TEACH: How?]
BOB: I talked to her.
TEACH: You talked to her.
BOB: Yes.
TEACH: I asked you you weren't going to.
BOB: Well, she asked me.
[TEACH: What?]
[BOB: That you were over here.]
TEACH: What did you tell her?
BOB: That you were here.
[TEACH: Oh.]
```

Common Beginner's Mistakes: "The 5 Too's"

I read a lot of beginning dialogue in my screenwriting classes, and much of what is wrong falls into five categories: Too much, Too formal, Too chatty, Too repetitive, Too "on the nose."

- *Too much.* There is just too much dialogue, as much as twice or three times more than necessary. Playwrights suffer from this problem because they are trained to develop stories via dialogue, and slowly at that. For the screenwriter, dialogue is a secondary, not primary, tool, always second fiddle to visual storytelling. Look for ways to tell your story without dialogue. Ask yourself, if this was a silent movie, how would I tell it? Keep dialogue to what is functional and necessary. All dialogue must move the story forward or reveal new aspects of character.

- *Too formal.* Write dialogue the way people actually talk. Dialogue is to be heard, not read, and there is a great difference. For example, we usually speak in contractions: I can't, I won't. If you write "I cannot" or "will not", you have to know what you are doing. People commonly only speak this way for emphasis, and the context of the scene must justify this. Learn how people actually speak by improving your eavesdropping skills. And read your dialogue aloud. Better yet, record it, preferably in someone else's voice, then listen to it. Dialogue that is too formal registers in the ear before it registers on the eye.

- *Too chatty.* Chatty dialogue goes nowhere. It may sound like real folks—but it does not move the story along. In this most efficient of all narrative forms, you don't have time to give us chat. All scenes suggesting chat must have a strong function in characterization or dramatic relief (like the dialogue relief after strong violence in a Tarantino movie). Chatty dialogue often occurs at the beginning of a scene—a lot of "hi, how are ya" that is pure fat.

- *Too repetitive.* Dialogue that tells us what we already know bores us. When one character informs another of something which the audience already knows, we suffer hearing it all again. All you need to do is lead into the explanation, "John, you'll never guess what happened," then cut to a new scene after the character has been told. Another form of repetition is when all characters sound alike. Give your major characters "verbal prints." Have them use distinctive phrases and syntax. Again, eavesdrop on conversations for idioms you can shape for your own uses.

- *Too "on the nose."* Dialogue that baldly expresses emotion, that puts everything on the surface, "on the nose," lacks suggestion and density. It is the opposite of "subtext." At times "on the nose" dialogue is contextually appropriate—during a heated argument, for example—but beginners overdo this, turning characters into folks at confession. The story becomes heavy, simplistic melodrama. In real life, we talk around our problems more than directly about them, and characters are more interesting when they do this as well.

Scene Design

By scene design we mean when a scene begins and ends. This can be initially challenging: beginning writers tend to start scenes too early and end them too late.

Starting too early means the action begins long before the actual focus of the scene occurs. When you study scripts and movies, pay particular attention to when scenes start— how quickly they put you into the middle of an action. Beginning writers often take forever to "set up" an action.

Similarly, once a scene has made its point (and every scene must be there for a reason!) don't linger—end the scene. Don't drag it on.

Because of this need for efficiency, few scenes run more than a page in length. Scenes over three pages are rare. This is not a rule but a general tendency, though there are clear exceptions in character-driven movies like *When Harry Met Sally* or *Good Will Hunting*.

Make sure your scenes cut to the quick. In my own work, I double-check any scene over a page for its efficiency—the longer the scene, the more carefully I check it for fat.

Scene Context

Scene length depends on context. Let me give you two examples.

A woman and female coworker decide to meet for a drink after work. The woman, who lives near by, wants to run home first to check her messages because her father is in the hospital.

How would you design the scene of checking her messages?

If this is all there is to it, you'd want to do it as efficiently as possible.

```
EXT. OFFICE BLDG—DAY
Jennifer and Gayle come outside.
          JENNIFER
     This won't take a minute. I'll see
you there.
She hurries off.
INT. JENNIFER'S APARTMENT—DAY
She looks at her message machine. Zero
messages.
Jennifer looks worried but doesn't make a
call.
INT. RESTAURANT—BAR—DAY
```

And so on.

Let's complicate the situation. Jennifer is being stalked. She doesn't realize this yet, though she's seen clues and is beginning to worry.

Now we can make the scene a page or more in length.

```
She hurries off.

INT. JENNIFER'S APARTMENT—DAY

Joe has broken into her apartment. He's in
the living room, looking at her cassette
collection.
Suddenly he hears something. Someone is
opening the door.
He looks around in panic. There's a coat
closet.
He hurries to it. He gets out of sight
just as Jennifer comes in.
She goes right to the message machine. No
messages.
```

But now we don't need to have her rush off or cut to the restaurant. With Joe in the closet, we have considerable tension we can build on. Jennifer decides to change clothes and goes into the bedroom to change. Joe comes out of the closet and spies on her. When she's ready to leave, he hides again. We've built a much longer suspenseful scene from the act of checking messages because context justifies the change.

Be aware of the dramatic context of your scene and design accordingly.

Examples of Scene Design

The Birdcage by Elaine May is a model script for scene design. A couple of examples follow below.

First example:

```
          MAN (rising to a very full
          height)

     Did you just call me an asshole?

          ARMAND

     No...actually, I was talking to
     the asshole behind you.

INT. ARMAND'S APARTMENT—DAY

Armand is lying on the couch. Albert is
applying cold compresses to his head.
```

```
                  ALBERT
          See? The swelling's already
          gone down. You were magnificent.
          Marvelous. Very masculine. I'm
          so proud of you. That big idiot
          looked so ridiculous when he sat
          on you and banged your head on the
          ground. He didn't even know how to
          box.
```

This is masterful scene design because the screenwriter knows what to leave out. We don't see the fight, we don't see the man sit on Armand and bang his head on the pavement. We don't see it because this is a comedy and such a sight wouldn't be particularly funny. What is funny is the quick transition from the instant before the fight starts to Albert's doctoring the loser, his partner. Because we are given no picture of the beating, our imagination is free to see the humor rather than the brutality—and so this moment becomes quite funny. The key to its humor is scene design, where one scene ends and the next begins.

Scene design also contributes to the efficiency and pacing of a story. Here's another example from *The Birdcage*. Armand decides to call Val's mother to see if she can help in the charade for the in-laws:

```
                  VAL
          You really think she'd do it? Wow.
          My mother ...
     INT. KATHARINE ARCHER'S OFFICE
                  KATHARINE (on phone)
          Oh, my God! Armand! I don't
          believe it! It's been a hundred
          years. Where are you?
```

We don't have to go through the decision to call her. We don't even have to see Katharine answer the phone. The cut is directly from the realization that the mother is there, and might possibly help, to her responding to Armand's call.

And that's a general principle behind good scene design: *what is left out is as important as what is put in.*

Subplots

Some people frown upon subplots. However, I think most objections are semantic. Subplots are secondary stories that give your script density and dimension. They may involve the hero, the villain, or other characters—but they work best when they are related to the central action, which will always be the case when the hero is involved.

- In *Jurassic Park*, a subplot is whether the hero's dislike of children will negatively influence his relationship with his girlfriend. Through the story's conflict, he learns to like kids.

- In *The Graduate*, a subplot is whether Benjamin will go to graduate school. Instead he takes his future in his own hands, rebelling against his stagnant middle-class background.

- In *Fargo*, a subplot is whether the heroine's husband will have his painting chosen for a postage stamp. When it is chosen for a three-cent stamp, the heroine reassures hubby that this is a worthy accomplishment, not only adding to the charming role-reversal of their marriage but ending the film on a note of normalcy after a pretty gruesome ride.

Antagonists, too, can be involved in subplots that run in counterpoint to the hero's journey. In *Chinatown*, Mrs. Mulray's escape with her child from her father (and the child's father) intersects with Jake's search for the truth. This leads to the story's climax—though along the way, we attach the wrong meaning to her story.

Subplots have beginnings, middles and ends—but you don't have to show all the points along the way. We don't see the judges in *Fargo* deciding the painting contest at all. This is a minor subplot used to "flesh out" the heroine by giving us small but important details about her marriage.

Subplots are added to enrich the story and broaden it into a more dense and layered reflection of the world of our script.

Pacing

Pacing is difficult, and even experienced screenwriters must work to improve their pacing. Pacing is about the ebb and flow of the story, the sequence of scenes moving from those that are gripping to those that are quiet, the big sequences and their interruption by smaller sequences.

Here are some guidelines that will help you develop a sense of pacing:

- To tell a story at only one level is boring. We need degrees of engagement—on the edge of our seats, then taking a breath; being surprised, knowing more than the characters.

- Big sequences need relief. Follow your explosions and car chases with quieter scenes.

- Tension must mount. Don't blow your wad too early.

- Pacing must increase jeopardy for the hero until we begin to sense a "ticking clock." By the final act, everything is on the line and there isn't much time. This is almost always true in all story genres.

- Think ebb and flow, rise and fall, with each new rise higher than the one before.

- Don't let indecisions about pacing stop you from moving forward early on. You need an entire draft in front of you before you can evaluate your pacing. Consequently, this is one of the last things you need to fix.

Visual Elements

Because we are writers, it is easy to forget that movies are not about language but images. Yes, a screenplay is a blueprint and the blueprint is in language. But this language, besides being economical and "minimalist," describes "moving pictures."

This is why the action element is so important. This is where you set down the "visual elements" of your story. As you complete a section of your script, flip through the pages and see how much consecutive action writing you have compared to dialogue. If all your pages are filled with dialogue, you have a very "talky" movie.

In *Boys from Brazil*, there's no dialogue for the first five pages of script— yet this is one of the most gripping hooks you'll ever see.

Imagine (again) that your script is a silent movie. That is, take all the dialogue out. The more your story still makes sense, the better.

Another practical reason to drive your story with action/visual elements is the foreign market. The foreign market loves visually driven stories because translation or subtitles are minimal.

"Movies are moving pictures" is up there with "American movies are about what happens next" and "the chain saw is your friend" as important screenwriting axioms.

Example of Visual Storytelling

I know no better example of the effectiveness of visual storytelling over dialogue-driven storytelling than the "dropping the gem into the ocean" scene near the end of *Titanic*. This is a completely visual scene: Rose comes on deck in her gown, carrying the gem, and steps up on the railing—and drops it overboard.

Compare this to the following long-winded scene from an early draft of the screenplay:

```
EXT. KELDYSH DECK

A desultory wrap party for the expedition
is in progress. There is music and some
of the (co-ed) Russian crew are dancing.
Bodine is getting drunk in the aggressive
style of Baker Joughin. Lovett stands at
the rail, looking down into the black
water. Lizzy comes to him, offering him a
beer. She puts her hand on his arm.
                LIZZY
        I'm sorry.
                LOVETT
        We were pissin' in the wind the
        whole time.
Lovett notices a figure move through the
lights far down at the stern of the ship.
                LOVETT
        Oh shit.
                                CUT TO:
EXT. KELDYSH STERN DECK

Rose walks through the shadows of the deck
machinery. Her nightgown blows in the
wind. Her feet are bare. Her hands are
clutched at her chest, almost as if she is
praying.
ON LOVETT AND LIZZY running down the
stairs from the top deck, hauling ass.
ROSE reaches the stern rail. Her gnarled
fingers wrap over the rail. Her ancient
foot steps up on the gunwale. She pushes
herself up, leaning forward. Over her
shoulder, we see the black water glinting
far below.
LOVETT AND LIZZY run up behind her.
                LIZZY
        Grandma, wait!! Don't
ROSE TURNS her head, looking at them.
She turns further, and we see she has
```

something in her hand, something she was
about to drop overboard. It is the "Heart
of the Ocean."

Lovett sees his holy grail in her hand and
his eyes go wide. Rose keeps it over the
railing where she can drop it anytime.

>   ROSE

>   Don't come any closer.

>   LOVETT

>   You had it the entire time?!

FLASH CUT TO: A SILENT IMAGE OF YOUNG
ROSE walking away from Pier 54. The
photographers' flashes go off like a battle
behind her. She has her hands in her
pockets. She stops, feeling something, and
pulls out the necklace. She stares at it
in amazement.

BACK ON KELDYSH, Rose smiles at Brock's
incomprehension.

>   ROSE

>   The hardest part about being so
>   poor, was being so rich. But every
>   time I thought of selling it, I
>   thought of Cal. And somehow I
>   always got by without his help.

She holds it out over the water. Bodine
and a couple of the other guys come up
behind Lovett, reacting to what is in
Rose's hand.

>   BODINE

>   Holy shit.

>   LOVETT

>   Don't drop it Rose.

Believe it or not, this goes on for several more pages before she drops
the gem overboard! If you understand why the final movie version so much
stronger than the overwritten draft, you are on your way to understanding
the power of visual storytelling.

Big Sequences

A movie's "big sequences"—sustained moments when we are locked into the action—are almost always visually driven. In action/adventure movies they are easy to spot, but they exist in other movies as well.

Indeed, some commentators believe that a good movie can be defined as a series of three or four big sequences linked by a coherent story.

Consider these big sequences:

- In *Jurassic Park*, the first escape of the prehistoric animals.
- In *The Graduate*, Benjamin's trip to Berkeley and stalking of Elaine before trying to win her back.
- In *Fargo*, the kidnapping of the wife.

So look for your story's big moments, and don't be afraid to pull out all the stops when you describe them. Movies are exaggerations of life, and in your big sequences, more than anywhere, you can turn loose and give your audience the thrills, suspense, tension, hilarity, horror, grief, and joy of a lifetime.

Most beginning writers are too timid, writing as if movies were "realistic." Both a movie's entertainment and its truth are communicated through exaggeration.

The screenplay's minimalist and meticulously ordered structure alone makes it "un-lifelike." Since you're not imitating life in the first place, allow yourself to stretch in the other direction from time to time, in those high-energy moments, those "big sequences."

Exercises

1. Select a description of place from one of your favorite novels. Rewrite the sequence for the screen.
2. Think of someone in your life who is "a character." List the things that lead you to regard him that way. How might you use some of these traits in one of your fictional characters?
3. List the big sequences in a movie you've recently seen.

9

YOUR HERO'S CHALLENGE
WRITING ACT ONE

As we saw in the last chapter, knowing certain conventions separates the amateurs from the screenwrights. Now we'll consider the distinct needs of tree people and forest people.

Pre-writing for Tree People

You already should have done most of your pre-writing activity with your paradigm chart and possibly with your step outline.

If you didn't do a step outline, you still may have work to do on your supporting characters—everyone other than your hero and villain. In the hero's journey paradigm major supporting characters are identified as "hero's helpers" or "villain's helpers," important supporting characters who must relate to the central conflict and be connected in some way with one or both of the major characters.

Your major secondary characters require as much thought as your hero and villain. If you haven't given them that thought, now is the time.

Pre-writing for Forest People

Pre-writing? What pre-writing?

Actually, even forest people stay awake at night thinking about their stories. So do yourself a favor and concentrate on "first things first."

Get to know your characters: hero, antagonist and major secondary characters. Be sure of the dramatic spine of your story. Think of the spine of your story in terms of its central conflict: *hero—goal—obstacle*.

These things can be created or developed in the very act of writing, usually the best creative environment for forest people.

Give yourself more early slack than tree people do.

Despite what others may tell you, that's okay.

Really, it is.

Doing Research

Research is another form of preparation, one often misunderstood. There are two kinds of research: exterior and interior. "Exterior" research is the obvious. If you are writing a story with a policeman protagonist, you need to know about the life of a policeman. How do you learn these things?

Recently, a writer acquaintance faced with this problem called his local police department, stated his dilemma, and was invited to spend time on the beat with a policeman. That's doing exterior research. You also can learn about policemen by reading books (particularly memoirs) written by policemen or by studying novels and movies about policemen.

What about a policeman's emotional life? You can interview a cop about that, but the most helpful information will probably come from your own emotional life. Interior research means looking inward and revisiting the highs and lows of your own life. As I often tell my students, your life is your best material. How would you behave if you were a policeman? The answer may give you more gripping drama than your more intellectual but remote exterior research.

A word of caution. Be careful not to force too much of your exterior research into the compressed narrative of your screenplay. Having done all this exterior research, you will be tempted to use as much as you can. Resist.

In the final analysis, your characters should ring true if they are based on your own emotional truth and perceptions.

The Hook

The first ten pages of your screenplay are very important. You must begin with great efficiency. Starting a scene too early will cost you dearly in the first words after FADE IN:

Consider *Kramer vs. Kramer*. Most beginning screenwriters would start the story by focusing on the bad marriage, letting us see an argument or two, setting up (rather than starting with) the true beginning—the moment the wife leaves. Her leaving is the moment to begin because the story is not about the marriage but about the father's relationship to his son. The bad marriage is the story's context, not its focus.

True beginnings don't need to be set up. Take great care to start your story at the right place—as late as possible without losing anything essential.

This done, consider how to make the specific opening scenes grab the reader's immediate attention. This is "the hook." Besides setting up your story, it must plant a question in the gut of the audience: What happens next?

The hook can be very effective when it is purely visual. *The Boys from Brazil* has a wonderful visual hook. We see one of the Nazis hunters tracking some bigshot Germans living in exile. All we know is that the character (not the hero but "the hero's helper") is spying on them and excited about what he's seeing. Not until he calls the hero to report what he's seen, minutes into the film, does the dialogue begin.

Yet we are now completely engaged and want to know what happens next!

Quiet stories can have quiet hooks. Benjamin, in *The Graduate*, is "lost" without plans for the future. All we know is that he wants to have a "different" summer, yet that is enough to make us want to know what is going to happen.

Other Examples of Hooks:

- *North by Northwest*: Thornhill is led away at gunpoint, a victim of mistaken identity.
- *Atlantic City*: Dave steals a stash of drugs from a phone booth, propelling the subplot that will inform the main story.
- *E.T.*: A spacecraft is on the ground, aliens collecting samples of plants.
- *Moonstruck*: Johnny is trying to get the nerve to propose to Loretta.
- *True Lies*: The protagonist-spy crashes a party by coming in under the ice of a lake.
- *The Birdcage*: "Where is Starina?" The star won't go on.
- *A Beautiful Mind*: Young math grad students at Princeton are challenged to use their brains in the fight against the Soviet Union in the early Cold War.
- *My Big Fat Greek Wedding*: A Greek father tells his 30-year-old unmarried daughter she is getting old and needs to marry a good Greek boy.

Sometimes big, sometimes small—each hook engages our interest and begins moving into the spine of the story.

More for Tree People (Hook)

You've already set down your hook in your paradigm chart, possibly in your step outline as well. Now it's a matter of translating this scene into script form. Don't be afraid to take a second look at it, however, and improve upon it. How can you make it even more engaging and more visual?

Try thinking of your hook as a sequence of scenes, rather than as a single engaging moment. Depending on your story, more than one "gripping" thing can be going on.

When you start marketing your script, people in the industry will ask to read it. "Read it" usually means about five or ten pages—and that's how long you have to grab their attention. So your hook is not only important to your story, it may be even more important later as a marketing tool.

More for Forest People (Hook)

As a forest person, you haven't done the early work-on-paper tree people have done. So you need to realize that you only have about five or ten pages to win the reader's dedicated interest.

That's how much time an industry reader is going to give you once you start marketing your script. If you haven't "hooked" your reader, that huge pile of other scripts on his or her desk will begin calling.

As you sit down to write remember how important it is that you get started with a bang. "Bang" does not mean "loud" but "dramatic," with a moment that pulls us into the story, or something related to the story, that utterly grabs our attention.

Forest people may also want to read what I say about hooks for tree people. And vice versa.

The Complication

The hook doesn't necessarily have to "hook into" the spine of the story. It can have to do with a subplot or even with atmosphere or backdrop. The hook in *The Graduate* is Benjamin's general situation—there is nothing relating to Mrs. Robinson or Elaine, though they will soon come to the center of the story. We have a young man just graduated from college who has no idea what comes next. Many of us can identify with that. Even if we can't, we have reason to want to know what is going to happen to him.

The complication, in contrast, should involve the hero—either indirectly or directly. In *The Graduate*, Mrs. Robinson makes her first move on Benjamin, starting the first thrust of the story. In *Jurassic Park*, a lawyer threatens to close down the park, requiring its owner to hire the hero (and his girlfriend) to establish the park's safety.

By the time we reach the complication, we must be moving toward the story's central issue, to be on the hero-goal-obstacle track that will form our dramatic spine.

Other examples:

- *North by Northwest*: Thornhill is mistaken for a spy named Capland.

- *Atlantic City*: Dave and Crissie come to Atlantic City, where Sally is furious to see them.
- *E.T.*: Humans arrive, scaring off the aliens—but E.T. doesn't make it.
- *Moonstruck*: Johnny's mother is on her deathbed, and he can't get married while she's alive.
- *True Lies*: A series of complications (guards, a woman who doesn't recognize him) forces Harry's escape.
- *The Birdcage*: Albert wants the security of a palimony agreement from Armand.
- *A Beautiful Mind*: John Nash is a social misfit obsessed with finding an original idea for his thesis.
- *My Big Fat Greek Wedding*: Since childhood the daughter has rebelled against her family and Greek background.

Notice there is no formula but a lot of variety. In each case the complication moves us still closer to the spine of the story. This is most obliquely done in *Atlantic City*, where our protagonist Lou is not yet involved. But we expect him to enter the story squarely at the call to action, as indeed he does.

More for Tree People (Complication)
Refer to your paradigm chart or step outline as you write this scene in script format.

Your script will be more cohesive and focused if there's some logical connection from the hook to the complication to the hero's call to action. Sometimes the hook stands apart from the spine, being a more peripheral moment that we nonetheless use because of its ability to pull the audience into the story.

But look for ways to keep the flow of early moments related. In *Jurassic Park*, a worker is killed by a prehistoric predator. Then the insurance man shows up, putting the park in jeopardy for safety reasons. Then the hero is hired to inspect and presumably endorse the park so that it can open on schedule.

One thing leads naturally to the other.

Your script will be stronger if you can create this same cohesive flow in these early, important scenes.

More for Forest People (Complication)
Early on, it may be difficult for the forest person, who does not have a written outline as a guide, to keep on track. Or, it may be easier now than

later because there are definite moments to establish early on: setting the hook (by page 5 or so), adding the complication (by page 10 or so), moving the hero forward in a "call to action" (by page 15 or so).

Moving from the hook, go immediately toward your focus on the hero. Look for a complication that will cause the hero to act or react—and in turn lead to the commitment to action that we call "the hero's call to action." The complication, therefore, is related to the dramatic spine of the story in a way that the hook really doesn't have to be.

The Graduate's complication occurs when Mrs. Robinson makes her move on Benjamin: "Take me home." In *Fargo*, it's when the anti-hero has the possibility of a deal that will relieve the financial burden that motivated holding his own wife for ransom. In *Chinatown*, it's when the real Mrs. Mulray shows up, proving that the "Mrs. Mulray" who hired Jake (the hero) was an impostor.

Each of these complications nudge the story closer to when the hero has to make a decision. Each complication leads directly to the hero's call to action.

The Hero's Call to Action

At the call to action, often just before the first plot point, our main character commits to the story.

In *Jurassic Park*, the hero gets hired to evaluate the park. In *The Graduate*, Mrs. Robinson makes herself available to Benjamin. In *Fargo*, the anti-hero has to go through with the kidnapping; the hero takes on the case. In *Chinatown*, the detective won't give up the case because his reputation is at stake—he declines an offer to have everything dropped. In *Nixon*, the President commits himself to the cover-up. In *Rebecca*, the future Mrs. de Winter goes to great pains to see her future husband one last time before leaving with her employer to New York—and this is the action that changes her life.

We know what the dramatic issue is by now—and the hero accepts the challenge.

Other examples:

- *North by Northwest*: Thornhill, almost killed in a drunken driving episode, is determined to prove his innocence.
- *Atlantic City*: Ever playing the bigshot, Lou intervenes to help Dave and offers his room, where Dave will prepare the drugs for sale on the street.
- *E.T.*: Elliot finds E.T. and decides to befriend him.

- *Moonstruck*: Loretta makes an effort to befriend Johnny's romantic and cantankerous brother, Ronnie.
- *True Lies*: Harry has the assignment to get closer to the woman at the party.
- *The Birdcage*: Armand's son is getting married, and Armand reluctantly agrees to cooperate with the wedding plans.
- *A Beautiful Mind*: Nash gets his original idea, to prove Adam Smith wrong, and writes a brilliant, original thesis.
- *My Big Fat Greek Wedding*: The daughter betters herself by going to computer school and taking over the extended family's travel agency.

Each call to action involves the protagonist in a decision to do something (or not do something) that will thrust him into the "extraordinary" world of the story. These out-of-the-ordinary circumstances are where the remainder of the story will develop.

More for Tree People (Call to Action)

This is the moment when the hero makes a decision whose consequences form the remainder of the movie. You've already given considerable thought to this moment in your paradigm chart and step outline.

Review the flow of actions from hook to complication to hero's decision one more time. If they seem inevitable, even though the hook and the complication have an element of surprise, then your hero or heroine is where s/he should be: moving into action, committing to a goal. At these early moments, there should almost be a sense of fate, a sense that the hero is destined to embark upon this adventure because this particular sequence of actions dropped into his lap.

Maybe they do so reluctantly, like the sheriff in *High Noon* who refuses to leave town with his new bride and decides to meet his fate against the outlaw coming to get revenge. The hero's call to action says something about the hero's character—something we admire—although at this stage this does not have to be a big issue.

The point is, certain things have happened—the hook and complication—that require the hero's response. That response engages the hero with the story, commits him to a goal, and he leaves his ordinary circumstances behind.

The story spine is now in place.

More for Forest People (Call to Action)

If you are into the flow of your script, that flow should lead from the complication directly to the hero's need to respond. This, in turn, becomes the call to action.

If this flow isn't in focus, your complication probably isn't closely enough related to the spine of your story. Remember the overview of three-act structure: *Put the hero up a tree. Throw rocks. Get the hero out of the tree.*

You are in the beginning stages of the first part: getting your hero up a tree, and that moment will mark the plot point that ends the first act. At this stage you must realize that nobody puts the hero up that tree; the hero gets there by his or her own actions or reactions.

No call to action, no story. Imagine Benjamin declining the affair with Mrs. Robinson, or the scientist refusing to visit Jurassic Park.

Writing without an outline, your burden as a forest person is to keep on track. You need to keep your hero front and center, which can be hard if your hook and complication involve other characters, as is often the case.

After your complication, take a time-out. Remind yourself what your story is about and that it's time to bring your hero front and center (if that hasn't happened yet).

The Act One Plot Point

Plot points drive suspense. When an action turns things around, moving us in a new direction, or a surprising revelation puts everything in a new light—we respond, "Aha!" or even better "Oh my God, now what?"

The hero, having moved into action, is now going to be hit in the face with our first major plot point, ending Act One. If there were an intermission here, we'd hang around to see what happens next.

- In *Jurassic Park*, we, along with the hero, get our first wondrous glimpse of dinosaurs wandering through the park. The hero has entered a new extraordinary world.

- In *The Graduate*, Benjamin begins his affair with Mrs. Robinson. In *Fargo*, the hero tells his father-in-law about the kidnapping and the need for ransom money.

- In *Chinatown*, the hero learns that Mr. Mulray is dead. In *Nixon*, Nixon drops out of politics.

- In *Rebecca*, the new Mrs. de Winter marries and comes to her husband's estate, truly a fish out of water.

- In *North by Northwest*, Thornhill is set up as the murderer of a U.N. diplomat but manages to escape.

- In *Atlantic City*, Dave is killed, leaving Lou with $4000 and the rest of the drugs. In *E.T.*, Elliot brings E.T. into his room and introduces him to his brother and sister.
- In *Moonstruck*, Ronnie seduces Loretta.
- In *True Lies*, Harry believes his wife is having an affair.
- In *The Birdcage*, Armand gives in to a charade to fool his son's prospective in-laws into believing he and Albert are not gay partners.

What do all these plot points share? The first act plot point shows how the hero acts or reacts, moving the story in a new direction. The future is uncertain. We have passed the point of no return; we are in a new world.

More for Tree People (Plot Point)

You should be able to script this scene, as you did earlier, right off the paradigm chart or step outline. But before you move on, take a moment to review your first act. If there are major problems, you might want to repair them before you continue. Minor problems can be fixed later.

Ask yourself if the reader will continue after the first five pages. Is more than one thing going on by page ten? Has there been a complication to the initial dramatic beginning (hook)? By page fifteen or twenty—preferably earlier—do we know who the main character is? Is it also clear (by 15-20 pp) what this movie is about and what kind of a movie we're in?

If you answer "no" to any of these questions, put on your editorial hat. Start fixing the script—or the paradigm, if you prefer to rethink with your starting tools—until you can answer "yes" to all of them.

Hopefully, you will have eliminated these problems while you were thinking through your paradigm chart. Hopefully, much of your writing of Act One has been expanding on the scenes already developed by your structuring tools.

That's why you're a tree person—to solve problems sooner rather than later.

More for Forest People (Plot Point)

If you took my structure "shortcut," you are writing in four files or modules. As you leave the hero's call to action, you should have only 5 or 10 pages left to turn your story in a surprising new direction.

As a forest person your guidelines are mostly internal, so pay attention to structural demands at each stage of development. This is why I recommended the "four file" approach—you have less to worry about at one time.

The plot point at this stage can seem to come out of nowhere—Jake discovers Mr. Mulray dead in Chinatown, for instance—but it must have dramatic justification later.

When the Greek playwrights got stuck, they dropped one of the gods down to fix things—what is known as the *deus ex machina*. That won't work for us.

Try to have a physical sense of your file/module's length as you write Act One. Once the hero commits to what will become the story, more than halfway through this part, you have very little time to introduce the act's closing plot point.

Forest people are more liable than tree people to go off on tangents. Sometimes, you may want to go with the flow, just to see if anything interesting develops. Remember, however, that you are bound by the constraints of an economical form and will have to justify every scene. These little excursions may not lead to useful places. If one does, you still may have to prune your work considerably.

Your Project's Act One

Now it's your turn, time for you to start writing your own script's Act One. If you have a busy life, arranging how to do this can be a problem.

I suggest the following:

- Look at the rhythm of your life and decide the time of day when you can guarantee yourself a minimum of thirty minutes.
- Commit to a time when you will write—at least every other day, four days a week.
- Stick to the writing schedule you've set up for yourself.
- Let your family or housemates know you are not to be interrupted.

Writing Tips for Tree People

Print out the paradigm chart and have it beside you at all times. Or double task, so you can easily bring it up on your computer and move between the chart and your developing script.

If you made a step outline, keep the index cards at hand, going through them one scene at a time as you expand the scenes into scripted form.

When you make changes from the chart or outline—that is, when you script something substantially different from your paradigm or outline—draw a circle in red on the chart/outline around the "discarded" scene. If you discover your first notion was right, it's easier to find the changes you made along the way.

Write "point by point" and think about what you need to accomplish in small increments—no more than five pages at a time. "I have the opening five pages here, and I want to establish that the hoods trailing the First Lady are preparing to kidnap her."

Be satisfied that each small part of your script—the hook, the complication, the call to action, the plot point—is how you want it before moving on. Having a chart or outline makes it easy to find out where you are. You're not going to get lost.

When you see yourself wanting to make major changes, stop. Go back to your paradigm chart. How will these major changes affect what follows? To produce the best possible script, you will constantly be seeking better ways to do things. You may find you have to start over. If you do, you do. Sometimes there's no choice but to go back and write a new paradigm chart.

From time to time, go back and review the basic skills to make sure you are writing with sufficient economy.

Try to write on a schedule and set a realistic pages-per-session goal. Write for a week and see what your average is. Don't set a goal that is a challenge but one that is realistic, that you can actually meet every session. Congratulate yourself when you surpass your goal.

Remember that "clay is not cement." Your draft is a draft. Everything can be changed. Don't be too hard on yourself right now. At this stage you need a cheerleader more than a critic. Though you can be your own worst critic—and should be!—save it for later. First, we want to get a first draft of your screenplay.

Keep writing. Accept the challenge of your task. Keep writing.

Writing Tips for Forest People

Because you typically work more "in the heat of creation," what you write can be much more fragile. Be aware of this and protect yourself.

Tree people, interrupted by the phone, can pick up the outline where they left off. As a forest person, you have jumped in and are doing everything at once. A phone call can derail your train of thought—and, with little committed to writing yet, that can be disastrous.

Here are some tips for avoiding such disasters:

- Create a work environment in which you will not be interrupted.
- Think small. Though it is your nature to see "the big picture," try focusing on what you are writing at the moment. Think in five-page increments. What am I trying to accomplish in the next five pages?
- Try to balance your writing "excursions" with staying on track. What makes your style of working exciting are those moments when the characters take control. But your characters are not

screenwriters! If their journey leads you away from your script, backtrack to where the journey began and try a different route.

- Review the basic skills to make sure you are writing with necessary economy.
- Don't allow your hero out of your sight (or "site"). Most scripts go astray when the hero drifts out of focus. Because you are working without an outline, you need to remind yourself to keep your hero center stage. Be sure you can justify every scene that does not have the hero in it.
- You are in a creative process. Give yourself slack to make mistakes, but sufficient discipline to abandon false leads.
- Congratulate yourself for the pages you want to keep.
- Keep plowing ahead.

As you write Act One, you can continue through the book or not, as you please. Some students do better if they move through the book slowly, waiting to finish Act One, for example, before reading the chapters for Act Two.

Others prefer a "first dry run" of all 16 chapters, coming back to do the actual writing.

Review: Focusing on Action

Once you have 25 or 30 pages of script, when you have Act One, give it a quick review before moving on. Fix what needs to be fixed, but abstain from a major rewrite, unless you are considering major changes in your concept. Part of the writing process (even for tree people) is learning along the way.

First, look at your script's action. Would it work as a silent movie? If so, your visual action is pulling its weight.

Look for white space in your action descriptions. Are you writing vertically?

Look for economy. Are the verbs working harder than the adjectives?

Are there places where you can replace dialogue with action?

Review: Focusing on Character

Read your script a second time. This time, concentrate on character and dialogue. Does each of your major characters have a unique voice—or do they all sound alike?

Remember that dialogue comes out of character: a Catholic priest has a different vocabulary than a drug dealer. Look for idiomatic expressions to associate with your major characters, verbal idiosyncrasies, unique verbal fingerprints. One character may say "true blue" a lot; another may begin with "Let me think on that a moment" a lot.

Look at the length of your speeches. Cut wherever possible.

Remember that most people speak in sentence fragments. Look for ways your characters can make quick exchanges, rather than pontificating or rambling.

Nobody said this was going to be easy.

Clay Is Not Cement

Above all else at this stage, don't get discouraged.

Do not get discouraged.

Tree and forest people alike, you are writing a first draft. Whatever goes wrong (and believe me, many things will), it is not the end of the world.

You are playing God in your first draft—but you are creating a world made of clay, not of cement. Nothing you are now writing need be permanent—and much of it shouldn't be. This is a process. You are learning as you go, no matter how much or how little planning you have done.

The creative act is wondrous and full of surprises—even for tree people.

Not all surprises will help the script. But some will.

Writing is putting one foot before the other, one sentence after the other. Keep going. Think of Act One as a separate entity, a module, the beginning of a larger structure. You only have to write 25 or 30 pages of script.

That's not a lot. If you squished out all the white space and pushed the language into prose, you would have less than ten pages! You can easily write ten pages —probably in a week, at least in two.

Even if what you are writing is bad—even if you know it is bad—keep writing. Nobody is ever going to see this draft except you.

Keep writing.

And, finally, congratulate yourself.

You have a draft of Act One!

Onward.

Exercises

1. List the script page numbers in your draft where the main character *does not appear*. If it amounts to more than two consecutive pages, double check them to make sure you are not endangering the story's focus, which should be on the protagonist. Tighten up moments away from the main character or insert new brief scenes with the main character that retain focus while moving the story forward.

2. *For tree people*: Compare your draft to your pre-scripting work, your paradigm chart or sequence outline. Normally you will make changes in the heat of writing. Rewrite your chart or outline to incorporate these changes and keep your foundation material up to date.

3. *For forest people*: Since you did not begin with external structure, pay special attention to your story's efficiency and focus. Is it clear who the main character is, what the conflict is, the protagonist's obstacles and challenges? Clarify if necessary.

10

INCREASING JEOPARDY
WRITING ACT TWO (PART ONE)

Before beginning Act Two, review each of the four major moments of Act One. If you want, scratch notes on your paradigm chart or elsewhere—whatever works to keep you abreast of your changing notions of how your story will develop.

Tree people may have already worked these kinks out, and their charts or outlines should be in better shape than the less organized notes of forest people. But occasionally even tree people are swept away by their own writing and find themselves in surprising places.

We all work differently, and one of your first tasks is to find the method best for you. You do this by trying out all the options.

Looking Closely at Act IIA

Act Two offers new challenges. Many people—I am one—think this is the hardest part of the screenplay to write. Lew Hunter, former head of the UCLA screenwriting program, once called Act Two the "blue collar time of screenwriting."

The second act is as long as or longer than the first and third acts combined. It's where we "throw rocks at the hero." The challenge is to structure the twists and conflicts needed to engage an audience's attention through the long middle hour of our movie.

That's why we're dividing Act Two in two parts—the first half (A) and the second half (B). This is why some people refer to the 3-act paradigm as the 4-act paradigm. But even in two parts, we are faced with a long section of 25 or 30 pages. Let's see if we can break this into smaller units.

The first half of Act Two moves the hero from the beginning of commitment (the story is now in gear) to a point where there's no way out. I call this the hero's "increasing jeopardy." The stakes are raised.

Let's look at what happens in the movies:

- In *Jurassic Park*, the predators escape during a storm. The stakes are raised to survival.
- In *The Graduate*, Benjamin loses Elaine by telling her about his affair with her mother. He also raises the stakes by deciding he wants to marry Elaine.
- In *Fargo*, the anti-hero has to come up with more money; the stakes are literally raised. (The hero meets the anti-hero for the first time. The investigation gets closer.)
- In *Chinatown*, Jake gets hired by the true antagonist and also becomes romantically involved with Mrs. Mulray. Now he has a personal stake in the truth behind her story.
- In *Nixon*, Nixon reenters politics, gets elected President, and his paranoia gets to play in the largest arena of all.
- In *Rebecca*, the honeymoon is over and the new Mrs. de Winter learns her husband may be incapable of happiness.

In each case, at midpoint the stakes are raised.

There's also room to maneuver, again making a very important point: the paradigm is not a formula but a set of principles, a set of guidelines for telling stories with a beginning, middle and an end.

Let me give both tree and forest people suggestions that apply to both.

What Does the Hero Want Now?

Begin by reviewing the changes necessitated by the plot point at the end of Act One. The hero should be different now, if for no other reason than s/he has committed to the story, wants something, and is going after it. The story spine of hero-goal-obstacle is in place. The hero has entered the conflict armed with optimism and initial success.

But now complications appear. By this section's end, only 25 or 30 pages down the road, the hero fully appreciates the actual difficulty of reaching the goal.

The Antagonist Moves Forward

What makes the hero's task difficult is the antagonist. At this point, bring your antagonist forward. We may or may not have seen much of the antagonist. It depends on how much the villain participated in the hook or complication. As we noted, the antagonist may not even be a character. In *Nixon*, the antagonist is a dark side of the protagonist's character, making the essential conflict existential, a character fighting his own demons.

How we meet the antagonist varies:

- In *Jurassic Park*, we meet the antagonist at the hero's call to action, when he hires the hero.

- In *The Graduate*, the antagonist is more nebulous. Mrs. Robinson herself becomes the obstacle to Benjamin's "true goal," to win Elaine, once he realizes it (at midpoint)—but she is his summer lover in the beginning.

- In *Fargo*, the anti-hero is our "main character" from one perspective, and from this perspective the "hero" becomes the antagonist. Anti-hero and hero don't meet until the midpoint—when the ticking clock of the investigation gets wound. Before that, however (i.e., through Act IIA), the focus shifts from anti-hero to hero. In this sense, the antagonist moves forward.

- In *Chinatown*, we are duped into following a "false villain" who has been the victim of the true antagonist. But we begin to learn about the true antagonist (Mrs. Mulray's father) in this section.

- In *Nixon*, who is the antagonist? The "other guys" envisioned by Nixon's paranoia or his own character? The latter gives the story the feel of classic tragedy. Although we are always engaged in this sprawling non-chronological biographical movie (there are lots of twists and turns, and in the right structural places), it is difficult to pin down a conventional antagonist. I prefer to think the antagonist is anyone who disagrees with Nixon's vision for America. At midpoint, Nixon's paranoia gets to play itself out in the most powerful job on the planet.

- In *Rebecca*, the housekeeper represents the antagonist but also the dark shadow of Rebecca, the deceased first wife. The housekeeper now moves forward to upset the new wife by showing off Rebecca's superior wardrobe, then convincing the new Mrs. de Winter to wear a costume (for a ball) she knows will upset Mr. de Winter.

In each of these very different movies—purposely chosen for their complexity and creative use of the paradigm—the antagonist advances in the beginning of Act Two. This makes sense because the hero is moving into action—and without conflict and obstacles, there is no story.

"If you have a pushover for a villain," asks Stephen E. de Souza of *Die Hard* fame, "what kind of triumph is that for the hero?"

The hero's path into increasing jeopardy and danger has some initial success. Although you are "throwing rocks" at the hero throughout the second act, remember to save your "big rocks" for the climax in Act Three.

Don't blow your wad here. Begin small and build, each obstacle greater than the previous. And through much of this part of Act Two, the hero can be winning—until there's the midpoint plot point, which may reveal a new goal and new challenge for the hero. In any event, the stakes in the story are raised.

Intermingling Subplot With Plot

Subplots are secondary stories. Occasionally, they are almost as well developed as the main story. A subplot can move forward early in Act Two. (Again, this secondary story is preferably related to the central dramatic conflict.)

In *Jurassic Park*, the park's disgruntled computer whiz is selling dinosaur embryos on the side—and whether he can get away with it gets considerable focus in Act IIA.

This works, first, because it gives us a nice early, suspenseful, "ticking clock." More importantly, the whiz also has screwed up the computerized security system, and its complete rebooting is an important plot point at the end of Act Two, when for a moment there is no security in the park at all.

This subplot also increases the potential danger of the park's research, which makes the hero's burden (to endorse it or not) more important. Here we have a subplot involving a totally different character, yet this action has consequences involving our story spine.

What subplot(s) can you spin off your story spine to add dimension and interest?

Subplots also carry your story's message. Of course, you don't have to have a message, though all movies, all stories, in some way infer a value system. Many beginners are tempted to say something important about society. Attaching the message to the story spine, however, can be a disaster.

"Got a message? Send a telegram," Samuel Goldwyn once said.

An alternative is to put the message, social commentary, or wisdom, in your subplot. It's the one place where you may get away with it.

Ways to Build Suspense and Tension

Wanting to know "what happens next?" is experiencing suspense; wanting to know this so badly we can hardly stand it is experiencing tension. You'll do well to add as much of both to your script as you can.

Look at how suspense and tension are handled in our examples:

- In *Jurassic Park*, much of the suspense follows the predators' escape. How many people are they going to gobble up before they're recaptured? When the children are left alone in the large kitchen, and the raptors enter, the tension is terrifying.

We know where the children are hiding but the animals don't—and we don't want them to find out! Turning monsters loose is guaranteed to add suspense and tension, though obviously not all stories lend themselves to this device.

- In *The Graduate*, suspense is gentler—until the climax. We automatically side with Benjamin against the shallow environment in which he's been raised, and we want to know if he's going to find a way to escape it. When he falls for Elaine, we want the happy ending and consequently the more obstacles in the way, the more tension we're going to feel. This really develops with the "ticking clock" of the impending marriage in Act Three. But note how a quieter suspense and tension works through the first half of Act Two when Benjamin goes to Berkeley to try to win Elaine back. We don't need escaped dinosaurs to want to know what happens next. Watching Benjamin stalk Elaine, listening to Simon and Garfunkel, works just fine.

- In *Fargo*, as the black comedy of errors turns a hare-brained scheme into an even bigger mess, suspense builds with each mishap. We learn one of the hoods is crazy, and whenever he's in a scene, we can't help but wonder what atrocity he's going to commit next. A character can be a walking a time bomb, the same way as a plot can be a ticking clock.

- In *Chinatown*, we follow Jake from clue to clue as he tries to solve the mystery at the heart of our story—but like him, we misinterpret everything until Mrs. Mulray tells us the shocking truth, "She's my sister, she's my daughter, she's my sister, she's my daughter ..."

- In *Nixon*, there are no surprises because most of the audience already know the story. The ingenious construction of the narrative drives the movie's suspense and tension (helped hugely by Anthony Hopkins' brilliant portrayal). Also, we see a "behind the scenes" Nixon (whether historically accurate or not, it is dramatically true) that even gets our sympathy, despite his law-breaking paranoia. We find him fascinating and want to know less what is going to happen than why.

Consider some of the following principles for adding suspense and tension:

- *Caring*: If we care about a character, we care what happens to him. If we learn something bad is going to happen, we wait for it—in suspense. If the agent of the bad deed enters, our suspense builds.

- *Evil*: If a destructive entity is set loose, everything in its path is in danger. Here it comes. Who does it get next? Suspense. Tension.

- *Anticipation*: When we know something the character doesn't know, suspense and tension build to the degree that the character comes to learn what we already know. A burglar is robbing an apartment. Oops, here comes the owner. The burglar hides. We know where. The owner moves closer and closer to the hiding place. Suspense and increasing tension.

- *Playing the audience*: Don't deliver all the facts at once—give the audience a nibble at a time, keeping them hooked. Alfred Hitchcock once commented, "The person who tells you everything about themselves right away is a bore." Engage the audience by keeping them from things they want to know.

- *Surprise*: A character walks down street. Someone jumps out of the bushes with a knife. Shock and surprise—and now tension, as the conflict becomes immediate.

- *Conflict*: Anyone who threatens the welfare of the hero, about whom we must care, creates tension because we want to see the hero win.

- *Rematch*: When the hero doesn't win, we want a rematch. We want the hero to win in the end. An earlier loss can increase the suspense and tension leading to final victory.

The Midpoint Plot Point

If the purpose of Act One is to commit the hero to the task that defines the spine of the story, the purpose of Act IIA is to bring the hero to the realization that it will be one hell of a battle.

After some early confidence and initial success, the hero meets the midpoint plot point and gets some kind of slap in the face. Maybe it's a temporary setback, maybe it's a revelation leading to a new track or even a new goal—something that again raises the stakes and the uncertainty.

This realization can be magnified and clarified by a better sense of the antagonist, as well as by a subplot or two that adds density and complexity. This section prepares us for the long and high-energy ride that will be the last half of the screenplay.

Again, the secret is to organize Act IIA as a module within the overall screenplay. Understand what this section needs to accomplish within the entire framework of your entire story—and focus on getting the job done.

Later you'll want to take a wider point of view. For now, writing your first draft, just focus on the job at hand—bring the hero to a realization that there is more to the task at hand than first thought.

Here are some examples of the midpoint plot point:

- *North by Northwest*: Thornhill learns that Eve, whom he meets on a train and becomes attracted to, is working for the people out to get him (58 min.).

- *Atlantic City*: Lou fails to protect Sally from the thugs after their drugs (68 min.).

- *E.T.*: E.T. communicates that he wants to go home (53 min.).

- *Moonstruck*: Loretta, after trying to dismiss Ronnie, gives in to her feelings for him (68-77 min.).

- *True Lies*: Harry kidnaps his wife incognito and, matching charade with charade, gets her to work as a spy (68-72 min.).

- *The Birdcage*: The son's real mother will stand in as Armand's wife during the visit by the conservative future in-laws (55-7 min.).

- *A Beautiful Mind*: As the secret work becomes more dangerous than anticipated, Nash gets more paranoid and erratic – until he's finally institutionalized. There we learn that the foregoing story is his hallucination – there is no spy work for the Defense Department! The characters we've seen are figments of his imagination.

- *My Big Fat Greek Wedding*: The love interest asks the daughter to marry him – and although he's not Greek, she says yes.

The midpoint twists the story in a new direction. Along the way, jeopardy and tension increase in a spiral toward the end of Act Two.

More for Tree People (Midpoint)

Always review the work you've written before going on to the next section—that includes your preparatory work in your paradigm chart and your step outline. Be sure you stay on your story's wavelength.

From this point, a step outline becomes much more helpful than a paradigm chart because the chart only records transitional plot points. Some tree people who have not yet written a step outline like to pause and do one now, before beginning Act Two. If you feel lost, this may work for you.

Remember to keep focus on the hero. Here you may begin writing more scenes without the hero as you let us see more of the antagonist or introduce subplots, but never forget who the story belongs to.

Drifting focus is a problem that almost always can be traced to Act Two, where the confusion begins.

More for Forest People (Midpoint)

If forest people are going to get into trouble, it's going to begin in Act Two. Forest people are writing without an anchor. As the story complicates, the antagonist moves forward, subplots get developed, and it's easy to get sidetracked and forget what your story is really about.

In the wonderful heat of creation, as you add dimension and complexity to your story, never forget your hero belongs on center stage as much as possible.

One way to assure this is to connect the hero in some way to your subplots. If they don't directly involve the hero, perhaps they involve his friends—what some call "the hero's helpers."

Keep on track—even as you follow where the story wants to take you. If it takes you too far adrift, pause and say, "Well, that was fun," and back up and start over—and get back on track. Don't stifle your creativity—but don't be afraid to erase pages of writing if they are irrelevant.

Force yourself to keep your story on track.

Starting Your Second Act

You now are ready to begin your second act. Focus on the next 25 or 30 pages and review in your mind, or on your paradigm chart or step outline, what has to be accomplished here. Take additional notes if so inclined. Start writing, being sure to pick up the logic of the story where you left off at the end of Act One.

When you're done, make sure your hero has a new understanding of his or her goal—that the journey to reach it is more challenging than initially thought.

And take a break and congratulate yourself again—you're halfway there!

Exercises

1. Make sure your protagonist appears to be succeeding early in Act Two. The character arc rises in the first half of the act, meets a challenge at the midpoint, and begins to drop in the second half of the act. What can you do to strengthen the hero's apparent success early in this act?

2. Look at how you introduce the antagonist, whether as a character, a force, or a dark side of the hero. Make the antagonist complex if a character: let us see something human, even admirable, about him. Complex characters are always more interesting. How can you make your antagonist more complex?

3. Similarly, you can make your protagonist more interesting by adding a dark side. List the hero's possible dark sides. What actions can you introduce to reveal these traits?

11

AIMING FOR THE STARS
WRITING ACT TWO (PART TWO)

There's nothing as exhilarating as starting a new screenplay! You like your concept and hero. You have a great hook. You know how to set down the call to action and first act plot point—Act Ones can go so well.

Then comes Act Two. Once through the first half of Act Two, you feel the game has changed. Lew Hunter is right, this is the blue-collar grunt work of screenwriting! This is where you give up—or learn to write a screenplay. If the first act is the honeymoon, Act Two is the honeymoon in hell.

Your task keeps getting harder. In the last half of Act Two, you have to move your hero into the jaws of defeat, so Act Three introduces a ticking clock and a final confrontation, the "showdown," where victory is secured against great odds. In other words, the hero, in most cases, reaches his or her goal.

Keep in mind, that the energy of confrontation can be expressed psychologically as well as physically. We don't need a big confrontation with blood spilled everywhere. In character-driven stories, in many contemporary indie movies—*Chasing Amy,* for example—the confrontation can mean increasing fear, uncertainty, or grief.

Keeping the Hero in Focus

Here, as throughout Act Two, don't let focus drift from the hero. The temptation in the second act is to let the antagonist take over the movie. Good "villains" are so much fun! What is *The Silence of the Lambs* without its wonderful villain?

In bringing the antagonist forward in the first half of Act Two, there's the danger of leaving the spotlight on the antagonist, not returning it to the hero. This becomes an essential point of balance.

I have a little "trick" you can use to help you keep the hero in focus. I call it "casting yourself a superstar."

Cast Yourself a Superstar

As you write, cast your hero with a well-known actor or actress. Forget any realistic possibility such a superstar will play the role. This is an exercise.

With a superstar playing your main character, the rules change. Superstars demand Big Roles. They do not like being off-screen for a minute.

Nor does the producer, who is paying the superstar millions, want to buy anyone a free lunch. The producer wants you to work the tail off the superstar.

See what I'm getting at? You now have an obligation to construct your story so the superstar is in as many scenes as possible, thus keeping your story-focus where it belongs!

Try this little trick as you write Act Two.

The Rhythm of Tension

It's time to say something about pacing and rhythm. Remember you are building toward a climax in Act Three, toward the "showdown." You don't want to blow your wad until then. The story needs to increase tension, not diminish it, move toward bigger not smaller actions.

This means there is room for release from the conflict that is built earlier in the story (before the climax). Tension is often released after the midpoint, in a quieter scene in which the hero deals with his or her new information (the plot point). Perhaps a subplot moves forward briefly, a contrast to the spine of the story.

Before the last act, when action is frequently driven by a "ticking clock," you want to move in and out of intense moments, breaking up high-conflict scenes with smaller scenes of reflection or contrast. This "rhythm of tension" teases the audience into the unrelenting tension of our climax.

Into the Jaws of Defeat

Then we begin the slow build toward our final plot point, which will lead directly to the climax and final act, to the "showdown" and resolution.

This movement into "the jaws of defeat" may reverse what seemed like a sure victory. In *The Graduate*, Mr. Robinson shows up in Benjamin's room, pulling Elaine out of school and forcing her into marriage. Just as it looks like Benjamin and Elaine are finally getting together, just as we glimpse a possible happy ending—it's pulled away, thrusting us into a final "showdown" before we get what we want.

This is consciously playing with the audience's feelings—and it's done with great skill. This is a skill you need to master.

The Second Act Plot Point

This section concludes, then, with a final plot point that represents the low point of the hero's journey – which also shoves the hero into his or her last big conflict.

- In *Jurassic Park*, all power is shut off to reboot the computer system, dismantling security—leading to a final face-off with the predators. (However, the resulting climax is not totally satisfactory because the hero does little to affect the outcome.)

- In *The Graduate*, Benjamin races "the ticking clock" to find Elaine before she marries. Even though he is too late, he still wins her.

- In *Fargo*, the anti-hero flees the interview with the hero, all but admitting guilt. The hero tracks down the killers.

- In *Chinatown*, Jake learns that Mrs. Mulray had her father's daughter. But the father, the villain, is going to end up with his granddaughter in this dark film noir ending.

- In *Nixon*, even the President's wife turns against him, isolating him completely. Our ending is tragic, a man defeated by his own character flaw.

- In *Rebecca*, Maxim tells his wife the truth about Rebecca's death—but now may go to prison for it. The second Mrs. de Winter stands behind him to the end.

- In *North by Northwest*, Thornhill learns the truth—but also learns he has put Eve, an American spy, into great danger and takes it upon himself to rescue her against great odds.

- In *Atlantic City*, Lou kills the drug lords—and finally feels like a criminal big shot.

- In *E.T.*, the humans have captured E.T., and both he and Elliot are very sick. E.T. dies.

- In *Moonstruck*, Loretta tells her mother "everything is different." The wedding can't go on.

- In *True Lies*, the terrorists take Harry and his wife hostage.

- In *The Birdcage*, the son admits to the in-laws that his "parents" are a gay couple.

- In *A Beautiful Mind* Nash stops taking his meds and his wife is about to permanently institutionalize him.

- In *My Big Fat Greek Wedding* the father declares the marriage can never work.

In two of these movies, our ending is dark—not the usual Hollywood ending. *The Graduate* is probably the most typical Hollywood example cited because the sense of a "ticking clock" is greatest. The tension drives the last act at a frantic pace, and Benjamin gets what he wants at the last possible moment, letting our lovers take the bus into the sunset.

The burden of this section of the screenplay is clear: move the hero to his or her greatest danger yet, and prepare for the climax.

Finishing Your Second Act

Once again, it's your turn.

Finish your draft of Act Two. As you write, keep looking for your hero—is s/he still the focus? Are you building in intensity so when you finish this 25 to 30 page section, your hero is as "defeated" and "down" as we are likely to see him?

Keep putting one foot before the other until you finish Act Two.

As always, congratulate yourself!

An Act Two Checklist

After you've celebrated finishing another section of your script, go back and ask some basic questions about your entire Act Two:

- Does the act begin by spinning off the twist that was the plot point at the end of Act One?
- Do we see the hero making some kind of adjustment because of that twist? Usually this involves moving into the new "extraordinary" world of the story, leaving the "ordinary" world behind.
- Do we get a better sense of the person, people, or forces standing between the hero and his or her goal?
- Are you still following all the basic skills of screenwriting?
- Despite bringing the antagonist forward, is the hero still the story's clear focus? In particular, do you have no more than five consecutive pages in which the hero does not appear? If so, can you justify them?
- Is there another twist midway through the second act, a major plot point that again demands a reaction from the hero?
- Does the hero see a "new goal," or the old goal in a somewhat different light or more clearly?
- Does the goal seem much harder to achieve than at first?
- Have you created a "rhythm of tension" following scenes of high tension with quieter scenes?
- Do the stakes continue to be raised through the second act?

- Is the antagonist a worthy opponent—is there a real challenge and contest here between the hero and villain?
- Are you moving in the direction of the end-of-act plot point, when the hero may seem defeated?
- Does the second act build and move toward the ending plot point that quickly spins off into a showdown between hero and antagonist? Is this all set up in the second act?
- Is the "ticking clock" ready to begin as you end the second act?

If you find weaknesses in the script, set them aside for now. Make notes—you can go back and fix things in the first rewrite. For now, since you are so close to the end, I recommend that you keep going.

The ending, after all, may take a new shape that requires much more rewriting that you now think. Writing is a process. Writing the first draft is playing God. It's the toughest part. In my view, the quicker we are done with it, the sooner we complete a first draft, the better.

Then and only then can we begin to do what is most fun: become a screenwright.

Exercises

1. Can your low point be even lower? How can you put the hero in even more jeopardy at the end of Act Two?
2. Does Act Two end with the starting of a ticking clock? Act Three will be more powerful if the showdown is urgent, racing against a deadline. How can you add a ticking clock to the end of your Act Two action?
3. Are your subplots resolved or close to being resolved? Act Three is going to be intensely focused on the protagonist-antagonist conflict, leaving little room to stray, so now is the time to tie up the dangling strands of the story. List your subplots and how they are resolved.

12

YOUR HERO'S SHOWDOWN
WRITING ACT THREE

Although you managed to get through Act Two, the longest and, many think, the most difficult part of the screenplay, the task isn't over. It's not as if it's downhill from here. We still have a lot of work to do. Act Three not only resolves the story, tying together loose ends, but must express the story's highest energy level or it will seem like a letdown. It also should send the audience home feeling satisfied. The protagonist should have grown. If you are very skilled, the audience may have grown as well.

Looking at Act Three

It helps to dissect the third act and to consider its parts—the beginning, middle and end of this section. Something happens at the end of Act Two that leads the hero to decide to act again, to recover from the low point of his or her journey, an action that spins into the final confrontation. There's the preparation to act, the action itself, and the consequences of the action.

Let me remind you that all four parts of the three-act screenplay can be dissected into beginnings, middles and ends—in fact, should be, to keep them on track.

- Act One:
  - Beginning: hook, complication
  - Middle: hero's call to action
  - End: plot point
- Act Two, Part One:
  - Hero's reaction to plot point
  - Antagonist moves forward, hero's initial victory; subplot(s)
  - Plot point, hero's insight, possible new goal
- Act Two, Part Two:
  - Hero's reaction to plot point

o New obstacles to goal; subplot(s)

o Hero's low point, possible defeat

- Act Three:

o Preparing for one last confrontation—the ticking clock

o Hero-antagonist showdown—gunfight at the O.K. Corral

o Resolution—the hero's growth

Let's look at each of these parts of the final act in closer detail.

The Ticking Clock

Some stories lend themselves to "ticking clocks" more than others.

- In *The Graduate*, Benjamin is racing against time to reach Elaine before she marries. He is too late—but wins her anyway.

- In *Jurassic Park*, however, we have yet another in a series of threats by the prehistoric predators. There is no more sense of a ticking clock here than in earlier attacks, nor is the hero directly involved in saving the situation. Some critics consider this a structural weakness—and I agree with them.

- In *Fargo*, the anti-hero has bolted the interview with the hero, so there is a sense of the chase.

- In *Chinatown*, the ticking clock is strong, regarding whether Mrs. Mulray can escape in time, with Jake trying to divert the police and help her.

- In *Nixon*, the President is trapped and squirming.

- In *Rebecca*, the new inquest seems headed to trap the hero's husband—a weak ticking clock.

- In *North by Northwest*, Thornhill tries to rescue Eve before she flies off to her death—a strong ticking clock.

- In *Atlantic City*, Lou and Sally are trying to escape but since the police don't know Lou is the killer, the clock is mild.

- In *E.T.*, we have a strong clock as the boys try to get E.T. to the landing site in time while being chased by the authorities.

- *Moonstruck* is not driven so much by a ticking clock as by anticipation of the showdown when the two brothers and Loretta end up in the same room.

- In *True Lies*, a series of action sequences keeps the plot in high gear but the impeding doom of a ticking clock is absent.

- A weak ticking clock informs *The Birdcage* as the gays try to sneak out the senator and his wife before the reporters discover them.

- In *A Beautiful Mind*, the wife stares at commitment papers for her husband, deciding whether or not to sign them – a mild ticking clock.
- Similarly the father's disapproval of the wedding in *My Big Fat Greek Wedding* is only a mild threat. The date itself suggests a ticking clock.

Where the ticking clock is strongest—in *The Graduate* and *Chinatown*, *North by Northwest* and *E.T.*—we are more on the edge of our seats. I urge you to incorporate this powerful element if at all possible.

How does one add a ticking clock? By putting a time frame around something we don't want to happen because it hurts the hero. The antagonist is on track, ready to win, unless the hero stops the action in time.

Thus Benjamin hurries to stop the wedding. Jake hurries to divert the police so Mrs. Mulray can get away. In both instances, the hero fails! In *The Graduate*, we still get the happy ending when Elaine goes to Benjamin even though she has just been married.

In *Chinatown*, however, Mrs. Mulray is killed and the antagonist, her father, gets to run off into the sunset with his granddaughter, a bleak and dark ending. Film noir is perhaps the one popular genre in which audiences readily accept unhappy endings. In *Body Heat*, the "villain" also wins.

Gunfight at the O.K. Corral

Then there is the showdown, the moment we've all been waiting for. This can be presented in a variety of setups and contexts.

- In *The Graduate*, the reversal from apparent defeat to victory —the "I do's" are exchanged just before Benjamin arrives—is wonderful. Benjamin pounds on the church window, yelling "Elaine!" Finally Elaine responds, "Benjamin!" A brief scuffle, and they are out of there.
- In *Jurassic Park*, the situation is the opposite—all gunfight and little ticking clock, little sense that this confrontation is any different from earlier ones, although the beasts are more formidable. The challenge in action movies is to avoid a series of actions that become too repetitious.
- In *Fargo*, the hero's confrontation with the remaining murderer is the gunfight, and arresting the anti-hero in the motel is dramatically anticlimactic, more a tying of strings at the end.
- In *Chinatown*, the "gunfight" kills Mrs. Mulray, the very "like Chinatown" ending Jake wanted to avoid. Once again, his attempt to help someone gets her killed.

- In *Nixon*, the gunfight is more psychological. Nixon, trapped and alone, faces his own demons, an ending appropriate to this "classic tragedy."
- In *Rebecca*, the gunfight is judicial and suspenseful. Will the truth be learned or not? The surprise twist, that Rebecca had cancer, lets the hero and her husband move on—but not without first witnessing the burning of Manderley, another vivid "gunfight" as the antagonist goes down with the mansion.

If the ticking clock is an optional element in your screenplay, the gunfight is obligatory. There must be a gunfight or a climax of some sort. This is the moment everything has been building toward.

Tree people will know what this moment is before they start writing—or at least be close. Forest people probably will not, trusting the "true ending," the "best gunfight," to reveal itself in the process of writing.

At any rate, don't be afraid to go for broke here and make the most dramatic and "big" confrontation your story permits. It's what the audience paid their money to see.

The Hero's Growth

The best stories have a point. The hero learns something from the experience, grows in some way.

- In *Jurassic Park*, the hero learns a professional and a personal lesson: that scientific research has its dangerous side and that he likes children more than he thought. Children are probably in his future with his girlfriend.
- In *The Graduate*, as Benjamin and Elaine bus into the sunset, Benjamin learns he can find happiness beyond the middle-class conformity in which he was raised. Or can he? With everyone on the bus staring at the couple, the ending may be double-edged, the comedy blacker than we at first realize.
- In *Fargo*, the hero and her husband learn to value life's ordinary moments—in contrast to the horror just experienced.
- *Chinatown's* lesson is bleak: Jake has repeated his past Chinatown experience. Perhaps he should stop trying to save people.
- In *Nixon*, there is no lesson: in this tragedy, Nixon learns nothing. His tragic flaw, his own paranoia, leads to his downfall, which seems as fated as the fall of Oedipus.
- In *Rebecca*, the hero grows into independence, finally able to build a life with her husband beyond Rebecca's shadow.

In some movies the character's growth is more obvious and important than in others. The paradigm is a menu of guidelines, not a formula. How much your hero learns and how you present this depends on the demands of your story.

Must You Have a Happy Ending?

Hollywood is married to the happy ending. This is a fact of life. If you have a story without a happy ending—and *Chinatown* and *Nixon* do not have happy endings!—you have a harder sale ahead of you. Be aware of it.

Hollywood is married to happy endings because we are. Most of us go to the movies to be entertained and uplifted, rather than slapped in the face with depressing stories about pain and loss, no matter how true.

But happy endings work best when they are earned. They are earned in the third act, when the hero overcomes considerable odds. The ticking clock is a wonderful device for driving the story toward the final confrontation, even more wonderful when the hero wins, as Benjamin does in *The Graduate*.

Yet some stories become artificial with a happy ending. This is why your movie's concept is so important. Here, this early in the process, you make decisions that will influence your ending. And the fact is, in Hollywood, the happy ending rules.

Bliss Is Typing FADE OUT: Finishing Your Script

As you prepare to write your own Act Three, first see if you can create the sense of a ticking clock. If you can, this will greatly help the line of suspense.

Next, make sure you don't fall into the disappointing trap of *Jurassic Park*, where "confrontation" is too much like what went before it. Use better models, where new and extraordinary action is introduced in the story's closing sweep.

Finally, ask yourself what your hero learns from all this—and show this to us rather than preach it.

An Act Three Checklist

When you have a draft of the final act, ask yourself:
- Does the hero enter the final act, after the second act plot point, realizing that a final confrontation is forthcoming?
- Is the antagonist looking more formidable than ever?
- Are subplots coming together to increase the tension in the main plot?
- Is there a sense of a ticking clock? Does the pacing now have urgency?

- Do scenes move quickly toward the showdown? Is the showdown worth waiting for?
- Are there a lot of visual "big sequences" in the showdown?
- Is the antagonist worthy of the hero?
- Is the hero worthy of the antagonist?
- Does the hero win?
- Does s/he learn anything from the journey?
- Are all subplots wrapped up?
- Does the audience feel emotion at the end?
- Does the story add up to something beyond itself—is there a theme?
- Would *you* pay to see this movie?

From FADE OUT to FADE IN: Preparing to Rewrite

You've done it! The first draft of a screenplay is no small accomplishment!

Now your work can really begin. Before it does, however, reward yourself.

Take some time off, at least a few days, if possible a week, before you return to your script. You want to get some distance before beginning what I consider the most important part of the writing process, the rewriting.

When you return to your script, ready to rewrite, do one more thing before you begin: read the script. Try to read it "as a stranger." Read it quickly, from beginning to end in one sitting. Don't take any notes.

Just read it.

Now you're ready to start rewriting.

Exercises

1. If your story has no ticking clock in Act Three, list ways in which you might add one. Don't force this – urgency should flow naturally from the story's events, but sometimes you can tweak these events to add such urgency, most often to the benefit of the story.

2. How can you crank up your final showdown? How can you raise the stakes so the final confrontation matters more? List the possibilities.

3. What is the final image – the last picture on the screen? List images that might better summarize the story's impact and list ways you can incorporate such an image through visual storytelling.

Save these three lists for consideration during rewriting.

13

WRITING IS REWRITING

I admit I tend to prejudge my students by how they take to rewriting. Those who fight it, who believe they can get it right the first time, who defend every syllable as if it were written in gold—I don't expect these people to become professional writers.

Because writing is rewriting. Writing is REwriting.

A former student, Cindy Boucher, puts it perfectly: "I don't write well, but I'm getting better at rewriting all the time."

This is true of all writing but especially true in such a collaborative form as screenwriting.

Again, screenwriting is the only form of writing in which a major outcome is to put a "finished script" into "development" so it can undergo major changes. Anyone who has gone through the experience knows exactly what I am talking about. "Development" is not done with novels or poems—and it's usually done in a very different context with plays.

You write the draft of your screenplay. You rewrite it. Twice, four, five times. Finally it's ready to market.

You find a producer who wants to buy an option, who wants to put the script "into development." You have a meeting. In the meeting the producer lets you know what changes s/he wants you to make. In short, the rewriting isn't over, it's only begun. But with an important change: you now have a particular sensibility to satisfy. From now on, what the producer thinks about the script is more important than what you think about the script.

Let me share an experience to reinforce the point. Summer 1998: I received a phone call from my agent telling me that an independent producer wanted to option my script, *Between Heaven and Hell*. The good news was the producer had a track record; the bad news was that in a buyer's market, little upfront money was being offered. The agent suggested I sign the contract, and I did.

Between Heaven and Hell was a thriller about a 50-year-old English professor and William Blake scholar who gets a night with a call girl as a birthday present. He becomes obsessed with her, and she sets him up to take the fall for a scam. However, he's a quick learner about the seamier side of life and reverses the tables on her in the end.

The first thing the producer wanted to do was to lower the age of the protagonist to 30s or even 20s! This would change everything. I couldn't imagine the story with a younger protagonist instead of my naive, shy, aging scholar.

But that's what the producer wanted, so I started a major rewrite. He also disliked the title. I changed it to *Earthly Desires*, which he loved.

I liked the new version. The female antagonist, whom the producer did like, remained and so did the scam. But now the younger protagonist and antagonist ended up together—a dark love story embraced the thriller. I sent off the new script with high hopes.

The producer read it immediately and phoned me. He was shocked I had made such major changes. He liked this version less. We had a long, serious talk.

Then a startling thing happened. For the first time, he told me what he really liked about the script—its similarity in feel to *Pretty Woman*. He wanted a love story between a guy and a prostitute! We talked some more, and I followed his lead to suggest the same characters could be reshaped into a story closer to a romantic drama than to a thriller. Let's try that, he suggested.

So I changed the story again in a major way. No luck. The producer was not enthusiastic about the result. Meanwhile my agent, hearing of all these changes, asked to see the latest version. She hated it. Moreover, she called the producer and argued that our protagonist had to be fifty or the story wouldn't work. We won this argument when the producer's wife read the script and agreed with us.

Back to the drawing board, but now with my original older, shy protagonist. We still needed a new ending. To make a long story short, several drafts later I ended up with a version retaining the protagonist—and also adding the romantic element, in that he still ends up with the young woman. Finally I had a draft everyone liked: the producer, my agent, and me. I was close to the original concept, but with a better hook, a more driving narrative, and a new ending.

This is the convoluted and fascinating process of rewriting a screenplay. It can be quite frustrating. At times, the screenwriter feels powerless because s/he no longer has final say over the material. That's why I say that screenwriting is not a pure "writer's form" but rather a collaborative storytelling form. If you need total artistic control over your material, the closest you can come is to become a filmmaker and even a producer yourself, not just a screenwriter. Screenwriters in Hollywood have little power.

This reminds me of a joke:

> *A screenwriter dies and is allowed to choose between heaven and hell, after St. Peter shows him both. In hell, rows of writers are chained to desks in a room hotter than a thousand suns. As they work, their fingers are singed, and demons whip them with chains. In heaven: rows of writers are chained to desks in a room hotter than a thousand suns. As they work, their fingers are singed, and demons whip them with chains. It smells like an outhouse.*

> *"What gives, Pete? These are worse conditions than hell!"*

> *"Yeah," St. Peter replies. "But the work gets produced, and there's no rewriting."*

Don't take my word for it. Screenwriters share their experiences in two classic books, *Adventures in the Screen Trade* by William Goldman and *Monster* by John Gregory Dunne.

But we're ahead of the game. You haven't sold your script yet. You are still trying to write it. And this is the only time you're going to have a chance to get your screenplay the way you want it! Savor this moment and enjoy the hell out of the rewriting process because, if you are lucky, everything is going to change down the road, and you won't be calling the shots any more.

The Chain Saw Is Your Friend

Rewriting is about changing things—more often taking things out than putting things in. This is not to say that you won't be adding scenes – you will be. But the screenplay's economy demands that much of rewriting will be about paring down and fine-tuning.

Listen to what two successful screenwriters have to say about it.

"The main thing—after you have the plot established and the characters set—is pacing," says *Witness* screenwriter William Kelley. "To see how you can cut every scene down and lead one scene into the next as quickly as possible until you think, well this thing is only going to be thirty-three pages long, if I'm not careful. But, it'll never be that." (*American Screenwriters*).

David Mamet, talking about rewriting *The Postman Always Rings Twice*, observes, "It was such a thrill to have a good scene that's five minutes long and get it down to a minute and a half and make it a better scene." This is what Mamet calls working within a tight framework. (Quoted in *David Mamet: Language As Dramatic Action*).

Learning to put the chain saw to one's own work—work you sweated blood over!—is not easy. But your willingness to ruthlessly cut truly determines whether you have what it takes to become a professional. You simply must understand that the most important part of the process is rewriting and perfecting your script. More often than not, this will move it in the direction of greater clarity and economy—in the direction where you need the chain saw, not the bucket of glue.

Consider the following scene, written by a student:

```
EXT. ATLANTIC OCEAN—NIGHT

US Navy frigate in heavy seas with strong
winds and copious snow falling. The ship's
sails are raised and tightly tied. In
the center of the ship is a single stack
spewing thick black smoke. SHIP'S DECK
SAILORS in heavy winter clothing scurry
about tying down various equipment and
securing sail lines.

Like clockwork, the massive ocean swells
raise the ship high then dip it down to a
sickening collision with the next wave.
In unison, the sailors brace themselves
for the next impact of water that explodes
over the bow and washes violently across
the deck. The experience of these sailors
is clear by the grace of their movement
and stone faces.

A figure SHOUTING inaudible orders stands
out from the rest in his erect, proud
posture and casually holding onto a line
that leads up to the mid mast.

CAPTAIN JACOB MALONE is attentive to the
work being done and the safety of his men.
Captain Malone cups his mouth with his
right hand as he shouts, but his voice can
barely be heard.

                JACOB MALONE
        BOATSWAIN! Muster your men below,
        the deck is secure.

Unexpectedly, a massive wave forty feet
high rushes toward the ship's bow. Captain
Malone sees a YOUNG SAILOR picking up his
gear and who isn't aware of the oncoming
wave.
```

In the first place, this scene uses a format fashionable about a decade ago but not correct today. Just as importantly, the prose style is unnecessarily verbose.

Consider this rewrite:

```
EXT. ATLANTIC OCEAN—NIGHT

US Navy frigate in heavy seas with strong
winds and copious snow falling.

On deck, SAILORS in heavy winter clothing
scurry about tying down various equipment
and securing sail lines.

The massive ocean swells raise the
ship high, then dip it down to violent
collision with the next wave.

A figure shouting inaudible orders stands
out from the rest. This is CAPTAIN JACOB
MALONE.

          JACOB MALONE
     BOATSWAIN! Muster your men below,
     the deck is secure.

Unexpectedly, a massive wave forty feet
high rushes toward the ship's bow.

Captain Malone sees a YOUNG SAILOR picking
up his gear, clearly unaware of the
oncoming wave.
```

The rewrite cuts the scene by almost half without sacrificing anything important to the story.

I've written "the chain saw is your friend" on a slip of paper and tacked it on the wall in my workspace. It's the best advice I ever gave myself.

The Forest for Tree People

I encourage my students to put on a different hat during the rewriting process. If you are a tree person, try to look at the script through the eyes of a forest person.

Tree people are in danger of over-planning until their story is too pat. Remember, the urgency to know "what happens next?" must also lead to genuine surprises. If everything is mapped out too carefully, too logically, the reader may be right in step with you and not be surprised at all.

When you are rewriting, try it from a forest person's perspective: writing scenes that are fresh and spontaneous, transitions that are surprising and even daring.

The wonderful thing about rewriting is you face the story with a comfortable security blanket—the first draft itself. You've already performed the miracle – creating something from nothing, playing God, creating the clay from which the earth will be formed.

Once that clay exists, no interruption is going to harm it. You can be more methodical and experimental, no longer playing God but her right-hand craftsman, the sculptor who is going to give this mound of clay meaning and shape.

So try to come to the material from different angles.

The Trees for Forest People

Likewise, forest people can now look at the script from a traditional structural viewpoint, donning the hat of a tree person. The story drove you through the draft. Now look at the script analytically and consider it from the three-act paradigm perspective.

Don't feel you must make changes just to fit the paradigm! Instead realize that the paradigm is a cultural preference for how stories are told. Look for ways to beef up the major plot points so they give the story more movement, suspense, and surprise.

I usually write wearing both hats: I often begin as a forest person aided by the slightest scribbling of a three-act paradigm, a rough sense of my three major plot points. I let the story take me where it wants, frequently checking that my hero is driving the story and not someone else. When I get off track, I make a note but continue ahead. The purpose is to finish a draft as soon as possible. When I finish a draft, and after letting it sit for a bit, I come back and read it as a reader/viewer—then I begin to think about my story as a tree person.

You might say that I write as a forest person and rewrite as a tree person.

Revisualizing Your Story

In preparing to direct his first movie from his screenplay, *House of Games*, David Mamet reflected that "the audience will understand the story through the medium of pictures, and the movie will be as good or bad as the story I wrote. That was the task I set myself in preparation: to reduce the script, a fairly verbal psychological thriller, to a silent movie."

Reducing the script to a silent movie is a very fruitful exercise. Read it "visually," disregarding the dialogue and focusing on what you see on the screen of your mind's eye.

A warning: this does not mean directing the film! This is not an exercise that will bring camera angles into the script!

This exercise is intended to trace the physical, visible action of your story line and to find ways to strengthen it. Where your story fails as a "silent movie" suggests places you might improve its visual communication – not in "directorial" ways but in the more general sweep of your story's action. Italian director Lina Wertmuller *(Swept Away, Seven Beauties)* does this exercise to good effect. Rick Schmidt describes her method in his fine book, *Feature Filmmaking at Used-Car Prices*:

> Italian director Lina Wertmuller ... takes a completed screenplay and rewrites every scene without any dialogue. She replaces her dialogue with visual storytelling, using images instead of words. Then she does a final draft of the script, a conglomerate of the most successful images she invented for the story (that replaced dialogue now no longer necessary) and whatever dialogue must remain for the story line. In this way she insures that her films will be first and foremost visual experiences.

Motion pictures are pictures in motion. Your blueprint is going to tell a story in moving pictures. Dialogue should support and reinforce that story, not the other way around.

Never a Wasted Moment

Rewriting can get confusing because you are looking for many things at once. One way to simplify the task is by doing multiple re-readings. Devote separate readings to focus upon your hero, another on your antagonist, yet another to read your script as a silent movie. Read aloud, listening to you character's voices. Are they individuals? And read with an eye on scene design and overall economy.

Be ready to defend every scene, every sentence, every word. Don't settle for less.

You are a kind of poet now. You write with Spartan economy because where you can, you use visual pictures—pictures in motion.

As you watch movies, study their economy. Even bad Hollywood movies often have good screen economy.

Does the Hero Grow?

Look at your hero at the beginning and at the end. Is there a difference? Has the hero learned anything and grown? The more confidently you can reply yes, the better your script.

But don't tell us your hero has grown: show us. At the end of *Jurassic Park*, the kids snuggled in the hero's lap are a picture worth a thousand words. Which is exactly what you're looking for.

Checking Your Protagonist and Antagonist

Consider the complete journey – the "character arc" – of your protagonist and antagonist.

Is the protagonist admirable and complex, with a dark side as well as a heroic side? Is the protagonist pushed beyond limits? Have you found an image that demonstrates the protagonist's growth like the sleeping children at the end of *Jurassic Park*?

If we haven't seen the true "evil" nature of the antagonist before Act Three, do you reveal it then? Is the antagonist a great challenge to the hero? Is the weakness of the antagonist a surprise, so the hero wouldn't have discovered it earlier in the story?

Does Your Prose Sizzle?

As screenwriters you are subject to a Catch-22. You want your words to leap off the page, involving your reader, but your rhetorical choices are limited. You have to make very few words do a very big chore.

According to director George Huang (quoted in *Big Deal*):

> "You've got to have such colorful prose that the words leap up. A lot of writers write to be entertaining. Other writers say, 'Screw that, I'll concentrate on what makes a movie.' You kind of have to do both. Think about the people who make the decisions. They're taking the script home for the weekend; they won't get to it till Sunday night at midnight. They're going to be sitting in bed, and if this thing doesn't absolutely rock and just jump at them from the page, they're asleep by page thirty....The spec script, especially, isn't so much a blueprint as it is a sales brochure."

Is the Audience Satisfied?

Finally, imagine watching your movie. How do you feel afterwards?

Are there things that confuse you? Are you left hanging and unsatisfied?

How do you feel after watching one of your favorite movies? That's the feeling you want.

If the ending is a downer, be sure the ride getting there was an exciting one, that the ending is the movie's redeeming reward. Other stories will leave the audience with smiles, tears, or wonder.

Is this a movie you would really like to see? If not, why are you writing it?

Don't get sucked into the trap of writing a movie—for money, presumably—that you yourself would not want to see!

Rewriting Your Script

Rewrite section by section, dividing the screenplay into the same four files or modules you used to write it. If necessary, review each section of this book before you start. Don't hesitate to review basic skills.

Set yourself a rewriting schedule and stick to it! Because you are rationally reshaping what is already on the page, you should be moving faster than you did on the first draft. How long did it take you to write the script? Cut that in half—this is your deadline for the first rewrite.

When you're done, set it aside a few days, then pick it up and repeat the process.

A Final Checklist

After each draft, ask yourself:

- Is there a compelling reason to read on after the first five pages of the script?
- Is it clear early on who the main character is?
- Is there a complication in the first 20 pages (preferably sooner) that calls the hero to action?
- Do we like the main character? Is it clear what the main character wants?
- Is it clear what stands in the way of getting it?
- Is there a twist in the action about 25 or 30 pages into the script, the plot point at the end of Act One?
- Does the hero seem to be "winning" early in Act Two?
- Is the antagonist moving forward in Act Two with a greater challenge than the hero anticipated?
- Are the minor characters interesting and compelling?
- Can we tell them apart by their language and behavior?
- Does something happen midway through the story—around page 50 to 60—to again twist the story?
- Does the hero learn or realize something here? Is tension relieved with quieter scenes to create a sense of pacing?
- Does the hero move into greater jeopardy at the end of Act Two, reaching a low point at the end-of-act plot point?
- Would a superstar want to play your hero? Your antagonist?
- Is a "ticking clock" introduced as we move into the final act?
- Is there a strong sense of impending conflict?
- Is the "showdown" in Act Three greater than anything that came before it?

- Does the hero win in the end?
- Is the hero changed at the end?
- Does the hero have a love interest? A close friend and confidante?
- Is the antagonist memorable—someone who really challenges the hero and presents a major obstacle to his/her goal?
- Are there several "big sequences" that visually carry the action?
- Is there humor in a drama? Serious moments in a comedy?
- Have you watched your script as a movie in your mind's eye?
- Does your script work as a "silent movie?" Does a lot of it make sense through visual action alone?
- Have you written with an economy of language?
- Are "power verbs" carrying their weight in your action scenes?
- Does the audience feel satisfied at the end? Did they get their money's worth?
- Does your story have a clear overriding theme? Is it bigger than the immediate story?
- Is this a movie that you would go see?

As studio or production company readers scan your script, they fill out forms that ask questions much like the ones above. The process is called coverage. They evaluate your work on a scorecard, reducing all your effort to numbers. Your final score often seals your fate. It's worse than grades.

Readers and Coverage

What do readers look for when they give your script coverage? Susan Kouguell, a former studio reader and story consultant, gives an insider's look at script coverage in *The Savvy Screenwriter*. She makes the following points:

- If your first ten pages don't grab our attention, it will be difficult, if not impossible to redeem yourself later.
- We want to see unique characters with distinctive personalities, that serve a purpose in the story ...
- Don't confuse us with extraneous characters ...
- ...actions need to be plausible!
- Endless dialogue and over-detailed description demonstrate inexperience.

- Don't direct your script with camera angles.
- Each separate action needs a new paragraph.
- Avoid heavy-handed exposition.
- Avoid rambling scenes!
- When we read voice-overs, we often panic!
- When we read flashbacks, our alarms start to go off!
- Incorrect format shows us you are inexperienced.

Screenplay Analysts

Growing interest in screenwriting has created a new professional, the screenplay analyst. Should you use one?

Before deciding, be sure you understand what a screenplay analyst may or may not be able to do for you.

A good screenplay analyst should be able to:

- Give you good coverage and feedback
- Show you how to improve your script
- Give pointers about your screenwriting in general
- If networked, and impressed with your script, possibly suggest where to send it

Don't expect a screenplay analyst to:

- Turn your script into an automatic sale
- Make the screenwriting life easier for you
- Get you an agent
- Establish your career

Analysts will not change your story concept—and producers say the concept is primarily what they are buying in a spec script. Analysts may improve your writing though they may not help your position in the market. No one has yet figured out how to "teach" good movie concepts!

What does this cost? It varies. Expect to pay at least several hundred dollars for such an evaluation.

Obviously there are good analysts and not-so-good analysts. There also are people taking advantage of the great interest in screenwriting—yes, there are sharks in the waters of Hollywood.

If you are considering an analyst:

- Don't hire one without talking to satisfied customers first.
- Make sure you have explored all other options, such as taking a screenwriting class, which gives you feedback but which also depends on the instructor's knowledge and experience.

- Don't hire one unless you are consistently rejected without positive feedback in the marketplace. In other words, query indie production companies (prodcos) before hiring an analyst. If I got positive feedback ("I like your writing but this one's not for us"), I wouldn't bother with an analyst.

If I sound a bit skeptical about analysts, I am. As a teacher, I know what I can and can't do for a student, and it upsets me that too many analysts are claiming something I believe is impossible. The good ones can improve your screenplay but they cannot assure your success or make your chore any easier in the long run. I recommend an analyst only as a last resort.

Staging a Reading of Your Screenplay

You'll be rewriting once, twice, three times—as many times, as many drafts, as it takes.

You can help yourself considerably by putting the script in the hands of actors. If you don't know any, advertise for some. Most newspapers in towns with a community theater have a "call board" section. Check your local college's theater department. If your town has neither, draft some of your friends and tell them, "Now you are actors."

By now you should have heard your script at least once—when you read it aloud yourself. Now you want to hear it in other voices, in a variety of voices.

It's amazing what you can learn this way. My play *Who Forgives?* received a staged reading on three successive nights at a new play festival. I used three different casts, tripling the value of the experience for me.

Readings of screenplays can be informal or formal. Do it informally first, with a group of actors or friends in someone's living room.

Then consider biting the bullet with a staged reading in front of an audience. This is a good way to test how your script works for the kind of strangers you are asking to pay money to see your movie.

After you've rewritten your script so many times that you think you can't improve it any more, take a breather. Let it sit a week or several. Begin another screenplay. Try to get some distance from it. When you look at it afresh decide whether to market it or to enter it in contests.

Meanwhile continue your screenplay studies by picking up some "tricks of the trade."

Exercises

1. Design the poster for your movie. This doesn't have to be "artful" but it should communicate the essence of your story. What have you learned about your story spine from your poster? Can you use this to tighten up your story?
2. Write the script for the movie trailer. What does this tell you about your story spine? Use this insight in rewriting.
3. Cast the major roles. Defend your choices in writing.

14

TRICKS OF THE TRADE

If you are serious about learning the craft of screenwriting, immerse yourself in how screenplays work, what makes them tick. This is something you'll be studying as long as you call yourself a screenwriter. Or a screenwright.

Meet as many people in the film industry as you can. If you live in North Platte, Nebraska, this might be difficult, but in a practical sense, a screenwriting career is about networking and who you know. This won't save a terrible script, but it will open important doors when you are ready to have them opened.

Don't miss opportunities like conferences and workshops to meet people working in the industry. Networking online also can accomplish this.

Read, Watch, Study!

The best way to learn how screenplays work is to read as many as you can get your hands on—and to watch as many movies as you can afford to see. An excellent approach is doing both at once: rent a movie video for which you have a script. Study the script and watch the movie with the script in your lap.

A reminder: virtually all published scripts are *shooting scripts.* Or, they were written by professionals who first sell their ideas before writing. In any case their format and rhetoric differ from *spec scripts.* Having sold the idea first, the professional screenwriter enjoys the luxury of being more verbose because now s/he is an investment. Thus published scripts are good models for storytelling, but *not for the format or rhetoric you will need to sell a spec script.*

Where do you get screenplays? Many can be downloaded online. There also are online stores where you can buy them. There are journals and magazines for screenwriters that analyze contemporary movies in helpful ways, interview screenwriters, or present useful industry news.

145

Let's say you have a copy of the script for *E.T.* I would use it to improve my screenwriting skills in this way:

- First, give the script a quick read, just to enjoy it.
- Next reread it, looking more closely at the people. Always remember that stories are about people (in this sense, E.T. is a wonderful person!).
- Then reread it again, paying particular attention to the three major plot points (Act One, midpoint, Act Two).
- Then put on the video. Use the clock on the TV screen or a watch. Watch the movie straight through the first time, looking for the major plot points, which should appear about half an hour, an hour, and ninety minutes into the movie, give or take five or ten minutes.
- Watch the movie a second time, following along with the script. Use the remote to pause a lot. Look for silent moments in the movie and note how they were written in the script. Look for differences between the script and movie (there will always be some since final decisions are made in the editing room in the film's terms, not the script's terms). Learn to make the leap from what you're reading on the page to what you're seeing on the screen.

Start a notebook or computer file so you can record the movies you've studied. Fill out a paradigm chart for each.

Your Life Is Your Best Material

"Write what you know" may be a cliché but it's true—and often misunderstood. Dostoevski did not have to murder anyone to write about the psychology of a murderer (*Crime and Punishment*). "What we know" has considerable meaning beyond the most literal interpretation of experience.

You want your characters to feel deeply, which means you have to feel, or have felt, deeply. Your emotional life is your best raw material. Next are the emotional lives of those closest to you. Another less popular but still useful cliché says all writers are spies.

Many beginning writers ignore their best material, because it is so close to them it seems unimportant. But ordinary emotions drive unforgettable stories. Look inside your own heart and you will find ample raw material waiting to be "fictionalized" into high-energy drama and comedy, mystery and horror. Your stories will be most human if you reach deep inside your own humanity.

Learn to mine the raw material that's so personal you've overlooked it. A dozen good story ideas pass you every day. You'll find them in your family, among friends, at work, among strangers, in the newspaper, on television, on the telephone.

I do not mean a literal "historical" rendering of something that happened to you, though we usually have a few experiences that might make for good stories. I am talking about your emotional life—the things that have made you laugh and cry and feel fear, horror, loss, hopelessness, pride, joy, confusion.

This is the stuff you need to give your characters to make them come alive. You've experienced such a range of emotions that you can dole them out a bit at a time, making all your characters different.

This is not always easy. Several decades ago I thought I was happily married until my wife decided she was a lesbian. The emotion that emerged from this experience festered inside me for another decade before it burst out as what remains my favorite stage play, *The Half-Life Conspiracy*.

Every character I write, no matter how small, is based on personal experience. How could I possibly put any words at all, except wooden ones, into the character's mouth otherwise?

Tom Schulman (*Dead Poets Society*) says it well (quoted in *American Screenwriters*):

> "From what I've seen, the people who just jump right into the full-blown fantasy feature as their first effort are kind of on the wrong track. To me, it's the simple stories, the stories as close to personal experiences as possible, that lead to the highest caliber of writing."

This is not to say your script should wear your heart on its sleeve. As a writer, you want to be a magician, to manipulate audiences without letting them discover how it's done. Structure is disguised by flesh. A script's foundation is only apparent when nothing else, not the characters or the story, interests us. In most good scripts we are so carried away by the people and their stories that we cannot discover the structure until we go back and look for it.

Similarly, the "self" in your script gets hidden and usurped by your characters. In a sense, you become every important person in the story. Your own emotional life in all its variety and nuances runs in their veins. Your characters' lives are real because they are about the most real thing you know, or should know: *yourself*.

Should You Join a Writers Group?

Writing can be a lonely business. In the beginning of a screenwriting career, isolation can be an occupational hazard. How can you evaluate your progress?

Well, don't do it by showing your script to family and friends—except in the rare instance that someone is a film professional who will give you a frank response. You need less flattery from people who like you than constructive criticism from someone who knows what makes a script good.

In fact, you need to learn how to become your own best/worst critic, who has high standards and who doesn't let you get away with less than your best.

Forming a writers group of your peers can offer one source of feedback. Ideally, a writers group would contain people who are equally serious about their craft. It also helps if several members have more experience than you do.

The danger of writers groups is that they can potentially deteriorate into ego-games. There are "professional" joiners who enjoy telling other writers how bad they are. There are others who tell people how great they are—angling for love in return.

Putting together a solid, workable group is tricky. I suggest starting small, with a few writers you can trust. Many successful small writers groups have formed online. You can exchange scripts and comments and even meet live in chat rooms.

In my experience, worthwhile writers groups are rare. More often than not, they become mutual admiration societies—but in the lonely world of writing, particularly early on, this is not necessarily bad. If you form or join a group, periodically review your reasons for being there, what you are getting from it, giving to it, and what you expect.

Don't use a writers group as a crutch. Hollywood is mean and stressful, and a "too nice" writers group won't prepare you for this reality.

Start a New Screenplay

Don't invest all your hopes in any one screenplay. No matter how good you think it is, you need to keep moving. It's the only way to stay sane in this business.

Especially after your first scripts, you may feel a powerful and justly deserved sense of accomplishment, and it's tempting to turn all your time and energy to marketing. But this is not all you should do.

This is why I suggest starting a new screenplay as soon as your first one is ready to send to contests, to market, to workshop in a writers group—or to abandon. If you know enough to abandon your screenplay, you indeed are learning something and are also able to evaluate your material fairly.

Most writers write two to five scripts before they have something ready to market. On the other hand, I've had two students option the first screenplay they ever wrote. For the most part, however, you don't want to enter the marketplace too early.

Beginning a new screenplay has another advantage. It will give you new interests and a more objective viewpoint when you return to look at the recently finished script.

In fact, I like to be working on several scripts at once, in different stages of development. I may jot down notes or fill out a paradigm chart for new ideas and put them away for possible development later. When I have a good draft, I usually begin a new script—so I am creating a new script and rewriting a draft at the same time.

Starting a new screenplay also reinforces the habit of writing. If you are serious about this craft, you need to complete two or three screenplays a year, in my opinion. If you are a part-time writer, this may be asking too much. But write at least one script a year.

So once your first is out of the way, make sure you always have two projects you are working on. One in creation, the prior one in rewriting— and down the line, the rest in marketing.

Screenwriting is hard work. Get used to it. Do what it takes.

The Zen of Screenwriting

If it's such hard work, why do it? What are the rewards?

Please don't reply—to make money! If you do, you are setting yourself up for disappointment.

Sure, many screenwriters make money—a lot of it! And I'll give you all the advice I can about how to make some of it—some of which I ignore myself because my values are different. I am from L.A. and will not return for all the money in LaLaLand, despite the strong professional advantages of living there. But there are other more noble reasons for being a screenwriter.

In Zen, poetry is not the words written on paper but the mode of thought in the poet's mind. I think screenwriters can learn something from this.

A script says something about the person who wrote it—what "mode of thought" produced the story on the page. If it's filled with racist and sexist stereotypes, if it's mean-spirited and degrades the best human qualities—I think that says something about the writer. I know this writer is not someone I'd like to have dinner with.

I am not saying film stories have to be highbrow. I enjoy entertainment as much as the next guy. There are some very entertaining scripts I wish I had written, such as *Rain Man*, *Cocoon*, and *Citizen Ruth*. However, entertainment and a kind of spiritual truth about the human condition are not incompatible.

I am suggesting you write from your best self. Realizing your own life is your best material—your emotional life, what you've experienced, felt, and know from the gut – gives the world your version of this truth. The most car-chasing, high-exploding, natural-disaster-packed visual high jinks can be improved by a little true human insight in characterization and story line.

Don't sell yourself cheap. See beyond the dollar signs.

You have important stories no one else can tell because they come out of your own unique human experience.

Tell them well. Tell them true. Be proud to be a screenwright.

Exercises

1. Start a journal to record the dramatic structure of each movie you see. Try to add at least one movie a week to this systematic study of screenplay structure and film storytelling.
2. Keep a notebook of your story concepts and ideas. Express each as a logline. Try to add a new movie idea weekly.
3. Begin a personal screenwriting journal, an informal dialogue with yourself about the progress and frustrations of your screenwriting education. Add an entry weekly.

15

Marketing Your Screenplay

At long last, you have a script ready to send out. Maybe it's your first script and you want to enter it in a contest. Maybe it's your third or fourth and ready to market.

You want to do a few things before you let your script out of the house.

Protecting Your Work

The first thing is to register your screenplay with the Writers Guild of America (WGA), west or east chapter.

Why? You want to register the script with the WGA because it is the industry standard. That's the only reason, but reason enough.

The easiest way to register with the WGA is online at *http://www.wga.org*. You'll receive a registration number, which will be used on a contract if you option or sell your screenplay. Until then, keep it in a safe place.

I recommend registering your script as soon as you have a final draft. If you make minor changes later – as long as the script is fundamentally the same – you do not have to re-register it. Registrations only last five years, after which you need to re-register to protect your work.

What about copyrighting? You may copyright your script as well, but actually your script is copyrighted as soon as your write it. So I wouldn't bother formally copyrighting it unless you are wealthy or very paranoid.

Preparing the Package

Although you register your script with the WGA as loose sheets—unless you register online—this is not how you present it in the marketplace. There's a professional standard that seems to generate a lot of discussion with beginning screenwriters on Internet newsgroups and mailing lists.

The standard is simple:

- Make a title page for the script. Title, your name, contact info. Don't put the WGA number anywhere because it dates the script.

- Bind your script between two sheets of card stock (65-110 lbs.), fastening it with two brass brads. Use a solid conservative color like manila, white, or gray. Nothing is written on the card stock cover. If you punch three holes in the card stock, which is what you'll do with the script's pages, leave the center hole empty. Or you can punch three holes in the pages but only two in the card stock. That way you don't have an empty hole on the cover.

- Use brads: round heads, about an inch and a quarter to an inch and a half long. Acco is a common brand; you can use the number 5, one and a quarter inch long, or a bit longer. Use the two brads to bind the script pages between the card stock covers.

- That's it: card stock, title page, script pages. No cast lists or prop lists, no synopsis unless someone asks for it, no budget, nothing.

The Pros and Cons of Contests

Okay, you've got a presentable rewritten screenplay bound between covers with two brass brads. Now what?

You seek validation of your screenwriting skills. One of the "safest" places to test the waters is a screenwriting contest. You won't burn any bridges if you lose—and you can burn bridges by sending out scripts to producers too soon.

Which contest? Before entering, you might want to consider:

How much is the entry fee? What does the winner get? Who are the contest readers? Who decides the prize? What is the track record of the contest? How many scripts will be entered?

In the beginning, it may be worth entering any contest, just to get your feet wet. But I recommend a more deliberate strategy.

There are two annual contests with a proven track record: the Nicholl Screenwriting Fellowship and the Austin Heart of Film Competition. There is the Columbus Discovery Awards, an ongoing competition with monthly winners and an annual grand winner. There are also competitions for internships or workshops, such as the Disney Fellowship and Sundance Lab, and some reputable smaller contests, like those run by the Wisconsin Screenwriters Forum.

I recommend that beginning writers enter the Nicholl and Austin competitions annually. The advantage is that winners sometimes (but not always!) move quickly on to screenwriting sales. More important to you is that by placing as a quarter-, semi-, or finalist in these contests, you open doors to producers and agents. These two entry fees every year won't kill you.

If you have the money and inclination to do more, be my guest. But before you do, listen to my warning and my alternative.

First the warning: beware of "fly by night" contests. A few people have figured out that thousands of "wannabe screenwriters" will do almost anything to break into the business, including paying fat entry fees for contests. Do your homework before entering. (One of the best resources for contests is at: *http://www.moviebytes.com*).

Get all the information you can. Pay particular attention to whether the readers have significant industry positions or connections. Remember that the quickest way any new organization can gain credibility is to give an award!

At $40 to $60 or more, entry fees add up. You might want to ask yourself if this is the best use of your money. If you live far from L.A., you could spend that money to get yourself an 800 number that might be much more helpful to your career. An 800 number encourages people to call you because it's at your expense.

Or subscribe to the online *Hollywood Creative Directory* for a year. The *Directory*, updated weekly, is the most up-to-date marketing resource next to reading the daily trades (which career-minded screenwriters will also do).

You need to put together a plan according to your needs, based on as many divergent opinions and recommendations as you can find.

When Are You Ready to Market?

When are you ready to enter the market, to write producers and agents?

One thing is certain: you should contact producers before agents. Why? It's harder to get an agent's attention because there are fewer of them. You do not want to burn bridges by showing agents scripts before you're writing at a professional level—assuming you can even get an agent to look at one!

You can accomplish a lot—even make some money—without an agent. You won't be dealing with major studios, but so what? You have to start somewhere.

But there are also beginning writers who get so paranoid about burning bridges they never enter the marketplace or do so later than they should.

In general, I suggest the following guidelines:

- Enter contests as soon as you want. There are no bridges to be burned.

- Compare your work to screenplays that have sold by reading as many as you can. (Early drafts are available at a website like Drew's-Script-O-Rama at *http://www.scriptorama.com*). Remember that produced movies have gone through an entire development process after they were purchased.
- Beginning writers usually need three or four scripts under their belts before they are ready to market.
- Begin with small independent prodcos rather than studios or agents. Your first goal is to get a reading from a producer.

Writing the Query Letter

Never send your script to a producer (or anyone else) unless it has been requested. This will mark you as a rank amateur.

First, send out "query letters," pitching the script and asking if a producer would like to read it. Queries can be by mail, electronic mail, fax, or phone. I discourage the latter, although a few writers with great phone personalities swear by this method. Most producers are too busy to take cold phone calls graciously.

The "standard" way to query is by U.S. Post. You are going to send out letters to the development executives at prodcos.

The first rule: keep the letter under a page. A variation on this is to do the actual pitch on what is called "a one-sheet" (a one-page flier pitching the script with a logline and short synopsis) and attach an even shorter cover letter. This is the method I prefer, but I have a track record, which means I have something to say in the cover letter. Most beginning writers will pitch and "cover" in the same one-page letter.

In pitching your script, your goal is to briefly intrigue the producer into requesting the script. This means you must have an appealing logline already written.

Below are query letters I've written to producers which resulted in a request for a script. One was sent to a particular producer unfamiliar with my work; another to a producer who had read my scripts and requested to be informed of my new work.

First-time letter:

Dear Mr. Jones:

I'm very excited about my new screenplay, THE SENATOR'S WIFE. A one-sheet is enclosed.

I've sold four options to independent producers, one of which is still active. I came to screenwriting from playwriting and have had over two dozen plays produced.

The public television version of my comedy CHRISTMAS AT THE JUNIPER TAVERN won a regional ACE award.

Presently I teach college screenwriting and am the webmaster of the Screenwriters & Playwrights Home Page.

May I send you THE SENATOR'S WIFE?

Letter to familiar producer:

Dear Ms. Smith:

Since you've been interested in my work in the past, I am enclosing a one-sheet for my new script, THE SENATOR'S WIFE.

Thanks for the consideration.

What happens when you are starting out and don't have much in the way of credentials? You put the pitch in the letter to grab a producer's attention.

Dear Ms. Smith:

Greg Apple has never gotten over his high school sweetheart, who is now the wife of a famous conservative senator. When he sees her at his high school reunion, he falls in love with her all over again.

To make the temptation greater, he learns she is unhappy and that she gave birth to his son after graduation. And now the teenager wants to meet his birth father.

But all is not as it seems, and "the senator's wife" uses Greg for her own purposes as she seductively leads him into a world of political blackmail, corruption, and betrayal.

THE SENATOR'S WIFE is a suspense thriller about a kind small-town man who gets sucked into the ugliness of Washington politics—but still manages to come out with his values intact. It's a political BODY HEAT with more brains.

May I send you the script?

I studied screenwriting at the University of Montana and have participated in a number of script workshops.

You want, of course, to beef up your credentials as best you honestly can. But a judicious presentation of the facts will help. Don't say, "I took a screenwriting course at Blah University." Say, "I studied screenwriting at Blah University." Both are true, but the latter sounds more impressive.

Keep the letter under a page in length at all costs.

Sample sale letter:

The following letter resulted in a reading and an option sale. After one year, the producer could not finance the film and the option was dropped. Only about one in ten option sales moves on to the next step.

> Dear (Producer):
>
> THE PARDON tells a story about the Vietnam War that has not been told yet. The screenplay is based on my produced stage play of the same name.
>
> Frank White fled to Canada during the war and started a new life. Now it is 1977, President Carter has offered pardons to men like Frank, and so he returns home as a widower with a young son.
>
> THE PARDON is a family drama proving once again that "you can't go home again" as Frank struggles to make peace with his father, a World War II hero.
>
> But Frank does prove to the world that he is not a coward when his son is taken hostage during a foiled robbery attempt, and Frank risks his life to save the boy.
>
> THE PARDON tells the story of a military family achieving a difficult peace long after the official treaties have been signed.
>
> May I send you the script?
>
> My screenplay RUBY'S TUNE is presently optioned. The public television version of my comedy CHRISTMAS AT THE JUNIPER TAVERN won an ACE award.

Again, brevity is key. Notice all the white space in the letter (short paragraphs). Almost everything sent to Hollywood is skimmed—a natural result of receiving hundreds of letters a day.

This, of course, is not an easy script to sell, being character-driven and having a hero who was a draft dodger. However, the subject resonates with certain people—and I was lucky enough to find a producer who was one of them.

Then he learned how difficult the sale was as well.

I still pitch THE PARDON. I believe it is an important story.

Here is a query letter by Adriane Rainer, a former student of mine. It resulted in over a dozen readings by producers, one of whom optioned the script.

> Dear X:
>
> I have adapted Kate Chopin's 1899 novel, THE AWAKENING.
>
> American born Edna Pontellier is a pampered young married woman who, during a summer vacation at the Grande Isle, falls in love with a vacationer, Robert Lebrun. This involvement leads to Edna "awakening," a transformation which causes her to question her role as wife and mother, and to more clearly define her identity as an artist.
>
> On returning to New Orleans with her French Creole husband, Leonce, and two young sons, Edna has an affair with another man, Alcee Arobin, and temporarily moves into her own lodgings. Such radical gestures threaten Edna's life as she has known it.
>
> THE AWAKENING was produced under the alternate title, THE GRAND ISLE, by Turner Pictures for cable television in 1991, to mixed reviews. I think you will find that my script presents a more powerful, compelling dramatic hook than THE GRAND ISLE, while remaining true to the spirit of Kate Chopin's book.
>
> In light of current public interest in adapted period pieces, a fresh take on this novel might generate excitement.
>
> May I send you my script?
>
> I recently completed a graduate screenwriting program at Portland State University.
>
> Sincerely, Adriane Rainer

A former student of mine, Cindy Boucher, rewrote a query letter that wasn't working and got much better results.

Here is her original letter:

Dear X:

I'd love the opportunity to submit my latest original screenplay based on the following premise, for your consideration.

"BEING NOBLE:" NOBLE MCALASTER struggles with the challenge of holding his family together in the face of his wife's terminal cancer and his own secret battle with a brain tumor.

Haunted by the thought he is responsible for taking away the kind of life his family wanted, Noble is driven to prove his love and himself. Noble demonstrates the quiet simplicity of lessons learned, sacrifices made, and the misunderstandings of love.

With your permission I would like to send the 110-page WGA registered screenplay for your review. Is a standard release acceptable, or is there an in-house one you would prefer? Thank you for your time and consideration. I look forward to hearing from you.

Here is the revised version, which Cindy says is "getting requests from agents as well as prodcos."

Dear X:

When you wish to prove your love for someone, is the motive selfish or selfless?

This is the question plaguing NOBLE MCALASTER in my latest screenplay, BEING NOBLE, which I would like to submit for consideration.

Noble McAlaster struggles with keeping secret a truth that could forever change his strained relationship with his daughter, in an attempt to demonstrate his love for his terminally ill wife. Noble fears if his secret is known his family will misinterpret his actions as those of redemption, rather than selfless love.

Set against the glittering backdrop of Las Vegas, Noble and his family discover taking a gamble is not always an act of desperation, it can be a statement of faith. Noble has little time to set things right, and for the first time in his life, he's not sure what right is.

With your permission I would like to send the 110-page WGA registered screenplay for your review. Is a standard release acceptable, or is there an in-house one you would prefer? Thank you for your time and consideration. I look forward to hearing from you.

Cindy has learned a lot about marketing in the traditional "school of hard knocks." Here is some of what she's learned:

The most important thing I've learned is not to market too early. The reputation of your work begins as soon as you send it out—make sure that first impression is one you can be proud of. Sure, be proud that you finished a screenplay, but realistic that just typing FADE OUT doesn't mean it's FINISHED. REWRITE until it is the best it can be, and then go back and make sure you can't do just a bit better. What you send out should be the best you can do. This way, even if that story may not be what is wanted/needed, if it is written well and in correct format they may request to read other work of yours. If it is not written well, you may never get another chance with that person.

The next item of importance in marketing is that the query letter must be professional, succinct, and such a grabber that the reader just has to request the script to find out what happens. It is for this reason I start with the names on the bottom of my TO QUERY list. I kind of test-drive my query with the first 20 to 25 prodcos, see what kind of a response I get.

And in order to get the query letter to your target market, research must be done. Be sure you address it to an individual, not STORY EDITOR or such. There are many directories out there—do research. In the beginning, I would send out queries rather blindly. The response was not great.

Now, as I'm writing I research prospective prodcos and agents. I read everything I can get my hands on in regards to this business. Think of how Melanie Griffith's character in WORKING GIRL researched—read everything and use common sense. Now, when I send out query letters I get a much higher request rate.

Some things to think about in researching prodcos: What types of scripts have they purchased in the past? (Check IMDb (Internet Movie Database), DoneDeal, or merely go to a video store and make a list of all prodcos that have done projects similar to yours.)

Are they looking into other genres? (read the trades and read/listen to interviews)

Are any of the execs (or stars they work with) making a public outcry regarding things such as domestic violence, guns, etc. (This is helpful if you have a script that deals with one of these topics.)

And keep a notebook with loglines that you wish to develop/are developing near the phone. The first time a producer called me in response to a script, I was so nervous I couldn't think of any of my other scripts to tell him about. BIG MISTAKE! BE PREPARED to pitch other scripts at a moment's notice.

Query Strategies

You should send out queries in great numbers. Don't send out one letter and wait for a reply! After testing your query, send letters out in batches of 50 or 100.

You are going to get no reply at all to most of your queries. Many writers encourage some kind of reply by enclosing a self-addressed postcard with multiple-choice selections: send script; not interested at this time; comments. I don't do this. I figure producers are busy enough without filling out forms.

Other writers enclose a self-addressed stamped envelope to encourage a reply. I don't do this either.

What I do, and strongly recommend, is include my 800 number for requesting the script. Many producers and agents are phone people (this is not an argument for calling them cold), and an 800 number invites a free call.

Let's say I send out 100 letters. What kind of return can I expect?

I expect about a ten percent return on "cold calls," letters to companies I've never approached, which amounts to about ten requests for every one hundred letters mailed. Other writers do better—but I usually write character-driven stories without car chases and big explosions.

When querying by email, this figure rises significantly to about 25%—over two times as great. Consequently, I do almost all of my querying by email. This means writing an even shorter letter that fits on one computer screen. (See below for an email marketing strategy.)

Not every prodco is a potential reader of your script. You need to do some research. The general rule is to identify the genre that your story is in—it's a little bit like this film or that, and then send queries to the producers who made those films.

But I think this is too restrictive. If a producer shows some production flexibility in choice of genre, then they go on my active list.

I tried querying by fax. It didn't work for me, though it has worked for others. Producers familiar with my work, however, have invited me to fax pitches of new material and sometimes I do.

Keep records! Keep track of what scripts went where and the result. There is software to help you do this.

Your most common response is no response at all. But keep those prodcos on your active list. Silence means "No thank you, not this one"—not "I don't ever want to hear from you again."

Others will say, "No thanks—but let me know about your next project." Put those prodcos on a list and call it your "B List."

Still others will ask for the script. Put those on your "A List" Depending on their response, put them on your "B List" to query again. If they like your work, make an "AA List."

Prodcos you've never written to before go on your "C List."

Many writers would rather write than market. You need to do both—and do both in an organized way. As you market your script, you also should be starting a new one. You should devote part of one day every week to marketing.

Marketing on the Internet

Marketing screenplays on the Internet is becoming increasingly important. Let me give two examples, one a free opportunity to pitch your scripts to an established production company, the other a paid service with an incredible track record.

Pitching Online

At InZide.com, screenwriters can pitch their scripts online. If the pitch interests a producer at the website, the entire script is requested, which is uploaded in Rich Text or another common format. No printing, no postage!

This is the way the Internet should be used by producers, and InZide.com is ahead of the curve. Whether this becomes a meaningful option will depend on the bottom line: whether producers succeed in finding moneymaking scripts this way. I am optimistic it will, because scripts from all around the world can be pitched.

Having used this website myself, I am especially impressed with how user-friendly and sensible it is. Initial pitches are in the form of loglines and limited to a small number of keystrokes. The genre is identified and the script must be registered, preferably with the WGA. You can pitch as many scripts as you like at no cost. When a script is requested, you hear back within a month (I've had three requested and passed on as I write).

You don't need an agent. You don't need anything but skill at pitching and a decent script to deliver as follow-up.

Exposure to Producers

The Internet is also being used as a script warehouse: a central database producers can browse. Ink Tip (formerly Writers Script Network) at *www.writerscript.com* charges a small fee for a six-month script listing. The script must include a logline and synopsis but can also include a treatment and the entire script at no extra cost.

Ink Tip has an impressive success rate. The website publishes a weekly electronic newsletter and each issue celebrates one or more success stories from the past week, an occasion of a writer finding agent representation or getting a script optioned.

This site's design is user-friendly, showing writers how often a logline or synopsis or script has been viewed, and by whom. The cost is very reasonable.

I believe online marketing options will increase, which will also help decentralize the process and make it less essential for spec scripts writers to live in Southern California. It should be noted, however, that full-time screenwriting remains a regional job. Most professional script work involves rewriting, and the assignments for them come from meetings with L.A. producers.

An Email Marketing Strategy

For screenwriters who don't live in L.A., I believe the following Email Marketing Strategy is their best option. It puts to use some of the marketing skills we've already covered in a special way. Over 90% of my students and former students who use the strategy outlined here get one or more requests for their scripts. This works.

OVERVIEW

In the strategy outlined here, all queries are done by email. It's a numbers game: the more queries you send, the better the results. You need to send at least 100 email queries to take advantage of this strategy. We begin by reviewing some essential first steps.

SCRIPT REGISTRATION

Before sending out your script, you must register it with the WGA (Writer's Guild of America), which protects your authorship. You can do this online at *www.wga.org*.

THE QUERY LETTER

This is your basic marketing tool. The email query is even more compressed than a standard query. You need to tighten your email so it can be read entirely *on one computer screen without scrolling*. Work hard on this.

A three-paragraph query is a good model:

- Paragraph one, a strong hook in a sentence or two ("Can the first female NFL quarterback survive in such a macho world?").

- Paragraph two, a tight pitch ("When the owner of the Stallions sees Mary, a cheerleader, throw a football for fifty yards, he concocts a halftime girls game. The crowd loves her and calls for her when the regular quarterback and his backup are injured. Mary suits up to play – and the rest is almost history.")

- Paragraph three, your credentials ("I studied screenwriting at Portland State University and am a published journalist. May I send you the script?") (The example is from a former student's script, which got many readings.)

RESEARCH

You next job is to find appropriate producers to query. Make a list of as many movies as you can that fill in the following sentence: "The producers who made [movie title] would do a good job with my story." Consider similar genres, visual styles, or any other reason you can think of. List as many movies as you can.

Next go to the Internet Movie Database at *www.imdb.com*. Look up each title. In the left panel, you'll find a link for production credits. Go there and list the production companies (not the studios) associated with the movie. There usually are two or more per movie.

The next step takes some time and needs to be done within seven days. Take out a trial subscriptions to the Hollywood Creative Directory Online (HCD) at *www.hcdonline.com*. This is the bible of the industry and is expensive – but a 7-day trial is inexpensive. So you need to do all your work within seven days, and schedule accordingly.

Look up each production company from your list in the HCD online. If they have email, copy it into a new list of email addresses. If not, you can write down the land address if you want to do a letter backup. This is not necessary since you are going to find lots of producers to query by email. Go through your list and generate an email list. Call this List A. Send your email query to each production company on the list. In the subject line of your email, write QUERY.

Now generate List B this way: there is a link in HCD that generates a list of all producers with an email address. There are over 600 of them. Open it. (*Note: As of this writing, this link has apparently been discontinued, which means you need to browse prodcos manually for their email addresses.*) Now go through each one (this is what takes time) and try to decide if they are someone to query. Look first to see if they make feature films (i.e. are not TV). Next look at their credits (movie titles) and try to determine if they are genre specific (some will be obvious makers of horror, adult entertainment, etc., from their titles). If you can't find a reason to eliminate them, put them on your email List B. Send your email query to each one, with QUERY in the subject line.

RESULTS

You should get at least a ten percent request rate – for every ten emails, one request for your script. Test your query letter first by sending out only 20 queries. Wait a few days and see the results. If you do not get a couple of requests, revise your query letter – make it more vivid and dynamic. Write it so that a reader *must* read this story!

When you get a request for a script, you will usually be asked to sign a Release Form provided by the producer. Sign it. They look scary but this is standard procedure. Send your script and release form to the address provided (to cover yourself, when you generate your email lists, also copy the names and addresses of the prodcos so you won't have to go back and find them).

Keep track of the companies asking for your script. These are the first folks to query with your next one. In fact, keep records of all your queries (for most you will receive … silence).

Then you wait. More importantly, *you begin a new script*. Never put all your hopes in one script. Market one, then go on and write another. My former students who are successful are the ones with the most endurance, not necessarily the ones with the most talent.

This is a marketing strategy that works. You should get readings. That's all a marketing strategy is designed to do – to give you opportunity. To make a sale, you also need considerable luck, which means being before the right producer with the right script at the right time. But it all begins with getting a reading.

The Pitch Fest

A recent phenomenon is "the pitch fest," where beginning writers get the opportunity to pitch their scripts to producers one-on-one. I witnessed such a "fest" and talked to writers who participated at the 2002 Screenwriting Expo in Los Angeles, where I gave two lectures and taught a workshop.

Although more conferences are doing them, I don't like pitch fests because writers are charged to participate. At the Expo, over 1,000 writers paid $25 to spend no more than five minutes pitching to a producer. I talked to beginning writers who stood in line over seven hours to get their pitch tickets. They did not complain—on the contrary, they were thrilled to have the opportunity.

However, the WGA, the screenwriters' union, will not endorse agents who charge reading fees because it regards this behavior as unethical. What's the difference between agents charging reading fees and producers charging pitching fees? Both exploit the dreams of beginning writers.

Fortunately, there are many ethical and free opportunities for beginning writers to pitch their scripts, particularly via email and on the Internet. You don't have to pay for the privilege of letting someone know how great your story is!

Your Turn

Using these guidelines, write a query letter for your finished script. Pay special attention to the logline and make sure you keep the letter under a page long.

How Do I Write a Synopsis?

The key, again, is brevity. And simplicity.

The length of a synopsis can vary, but producers will tell you what length they want. If not, do a one-page synopsis. I've never seen anyone request a synopsis longer than three pages. Also, the length preference often is a maximum length, so I suggest writing less – the one-page synopsis.

Write your synopsis in the present tense (with little or no dialogue) and give your story's highlights. Focus on the hero and the hero's character arc and journey. Write so simply that a teenager can easily understand what you have written.

Increasingly, producers seem to be asking for a short synopsis; it might be a good idea to include one with your script as a matter of course.

Here is an example of a short synopsis:

CASANOVA DOES CALIFORNIA
A screenplay
By Charles Deemer

LOGLINE (Romantic Comedy): An irate father gives the historic Casanova a magic potion that propels him to present day Venice, California, where he is appalled by his historic reputation, shocked by a porno movie being made about him, and falls in love with the psychiatrist who evaluates his sanity.

BRIEF SYNOPSIS:

Crawling out of the bedroom window of a young woman, Casanova is captured by the girl's irate father and given a magic potion that propels him from 18th c. Venice, Italy, to present day Venice, California. Casanova is immediately appalled by what he finds: scantily clad people and overt sexuality.

Appalled by the blatant sexuality he sees, Casanova quickly meets Christiano, an acquaintance from the old country, who was the young woman's lover before Casanova. Christiano has been in Venice (zapped there by the same irate father) long enough to know the ropes of living in the modern world. Still, he has been looking for someone with the magic to counteract the first potion and has a good lead on someone.

Casanova is excited about getting home as quickly as possible. Christiano is not so sure. He is portraying Casanova in a porno movie called 'Casanova Does California' – and loving every minute of it.

Casanova also is appalled when he learns what his historic reputation is, which he considers a disgraceful lie. Yes, he seduces women, but always as a gentleman, always with poetic style! He makes it his mission to set the historical record straight and to close down the absurd porno movie about him before he finds the magical antidote by which to return home.

In dress and behavior, Casanova appears to be mad – even for Venice, California! When early on he meets Henny, a psychiatrist, he falls instantly in love with her. Henny is engaged to a lawyer, whom Casanova thinks is unworthy of her.

Casanova courts Henny in the romantic style of an 18th century poet and soon wins her heart. She breaks her engagement, and they become lovers. When the lawyer confronts Casanova, Casanova challenges him to a duel.

Meanwhile, Casanova has found the magic to get him home. He tells the truth to Henny, who is very skeptical, still thinking him mad. Yet she is falling in love with him.

Casanova manages to close down the opening of the porno movie by leading an irate crowd to the theater. But he is not so lucky in the duel: he is wounded, apparently fatally.

Casanova seems to die in Venice, California, but wakes up in Venice, Italy, in his own time and place. A mad crowd has been chasing him, and a friend helps him catch a stage out of town. On the stage is the dead-ringer of Henny, and their romance is rekindled as the stage rides off into the future.

How Do I Write a Treatment?

You also may be asked for a treatment. In a synopsis, you tell what your story *is about*. In a treatment, you actually tell the story in the present tense with little or no dialogue. Frankly, treatments take as much work as writing a script and I only write them when I have no choice. Treatments can be short, five pages or so, but usually are longer, 20 pages or more. Here is how one might begin for the story about kidnapping the President's wife:

> The First Lady (Gwen) and her husband, the President (John), have been arguing during breakfast. Finally Gwen can't take his denials of adultery any longer and leaves the White House to begin her day's duties.
>
> Across the street, the White House is being watched by two foreign-looking men, Carlo and Andres. When the First Lady leaves in her limo, they follow in a battered old car.
>
> In the car, Carlo and Andres talk about this being the day. Andres loads a pistol.

The First Lady makes a variety of "good will" stops: at a hospital, a retirement center, a dedication. At each stop, Carlo and Andres follow and watch the scene carefully.

Finally, with the limo stopping for gas, Gwen goes alone to the restroom at the rear of the building. Carlo and Andres seize the opportunity – it's now or never.

Andres, gun ready, positions himself near the restroom door.

But then a customer, a woman, comes into view on her way to the toilet and, seeing Andres with a gun, screams. The customer turns and takes off just as the bathroom door opens. Gwen comes out.

Wasting no time, Andres grabs her, though the First Lady manages to scream before she is subdued. Carlo rushes to help, and the two of them manage to throw her into the back seat of their car.

An aide appears, gun drawn, and Andres drops him with one shot.

They get in the car and speed off, gunfire in their wake. They have successfully taken the First Lady hostage.

Contacting Agents

It is easier to get producers to read your script than agents. Many independent producers will read your script even if you don't have an agent. Producers of small budget films will also read your script if the concept interests them. You'll want an agent or an entertainment attorney if a sale results, but at that point you are looking for an agent from a position of power (though having a sale does not even guarantee getting an agent).

Eventually you are going to look for an agent. When?

It depends. If you are writing scripts that only major studios can produce, you will begin your search earlier than if you are writing character-driven or smaller budgeted movies independents are more likely to produce.

When it's time to look for an agent, the procedure is similar to looking for a producer. You can write a query letter. However, as agents are busy, their inboxes flooded, queries have much longer odds with agents.

Agents also look for different things in a query letter. Major L.A. agencies are interested in writers looking for a serious career in screenwriting. This means:

You have more than one script ready and are productive. You live in or can move to Southern California and can take meetings. You are more interested in commercial than "artistic" writing. You are a team player.

The WGA signatory list is an important list of agents approved by the Writers Guild who will accept query letters from new writers. Although not every agent lives in Los Angeles – there are writers who sell "spec scripts" without moving to L.A. or having an agent in L.A. – the farther you live from the action, the longer the odds.

Beware of non-signatory agents who ask for money! Legitimate agents will sign the WGA agreement, which prevents them from doing this.

You can get the latest "approved agents" list online at *www.wga.org* or by phoning WGA West at (213) 782-4500 (Information) and asking them when the latest list will be out. For a small charge they will mail it to you or you can get it online free.

Making a Marketing Plan

While you're improving your craft, you can develop a marketing plan. A marketing plan includes:

- A marketing strategy
- A marketing schedule
- A record of marketing actions
- A periodic review and revision of strategy

MARKETING STRATEGY

Your marketing strategy is a consequence of your goals.

Do you want to write big-budgeted action movies that the studios produce, the next *Independence Day*? Or, do you want to write smaller budgeted character-driven movies, the next *Ulee's Gold* or *Citizen Ruth* or *Chasing Amy*?

Earlier I showed you how to generate lists of producers and agents. Your lists at hand, decide the best method of approaching people: by mail, e-mail, fax or phone. I prefer email, postal mail second, fax last. I recommend disregarding the phone—there's too great a chance of interrupting someone during a busy day and burning a bridge. You want to come off as passionate but not ignorant of how busy producers and agents can be. If you live outside of L.A., use the "Email Marketing Strategy" covered earlier.

MARKETING SCHEDULE

Schedule a regular time when you contact the people on your list. I suggest one day a week. The important thing is that you have a schedule, that it's regular, that you stick to it. Whether weekly or monthly, marketing needs to become a habit.

What about follow-ups? I used to do follow-ups. I was very optimistic about my wonderful script, and knew people would love it once they read it. I had no idea my query was sitting on a desk next to hundreds of other optimistic queries. When I called to check on it, it seemed no one even knew they had it!

I no longer make follow-up calls. If that first quick reading of my letter, the only reading it's likely to get, generates interest or curiosity, I know I will hear from them—especially since I have an 800 number. I let it go at that and move on.

RECORD KEEPING

Record your marketing efforts in a notebook, or on your computer (using a Personal Information Manager or similar software, or in a word processor). Your record keeping should include:

What query letter went where and when. Whether you received a reply—and details about that reply. You especially want to know which companies or people request a script, which welcome hearing about your next project, and which are not looking for new material. If a script is requested, when did you send it and where? What results occurred from that mailing?

In this way, you start making "sub-lists" as I described earlier, indicating the people and companies most responsive to your efforts.

REVIEW PROCESS

Periodically review all aspects of your marketing strategy. If a query letter is generating no interest, your script may be a hard sell or your query letter may be ineffective.

I know writers who have revised their query letter, re-titled their script, and gotten readings from companies who rejected their first efforts.

An essential part of your query is your logline. Spend time making it as powerful as you can.

You want to review your marketing strategy because you want to make sure you are getting results. If you are not, something is wrong. Even with the "hard sell" material I normally write, I expect at least a ten percent positive response to my queries. If you're hitting less than ten percent, consider revising your query letter and logline.

The Development Process

What happens if your marketing efforts are successful? In most instances "success" is not an outright sale but rather selling what is called an "option." This is the first step in the script development process.

Hollywood's script development process has always been unstable and changing but perhaps never have writers suffered more than in the current "buyer's market."

Script development used to happen this way:

A beginning screenwriter would option a screenplay to an independent producer. This option would give the producer ownership of the script for a set period of time, usually a year, during which the producer would try to put together a deal with a studio to make the movie. Payment for the option was typically 10% of the selling price, which was typically 1-5% of the movie's budget.

A writer optioning a script for a low-budget 2-million-dollar movie could expect to sell the screenplay for about $60,000 and to option it for $6,000. A prolific writer could make money optioning scripts that never became movies.

Producers, of course, want to pay as little up front as possible, and the volcanic explosion of interest in screenwriting allowed them to change the rules. In the July/August 1999 issue of *Creative Screenwriting*, columnist Nancy Hendrickson summarized the dire results for writers: "With the spec market at a new high and development money at an all-time low, writers are getting more pressure to give over control of their material for little or no money."

An anonymous producer told Henrickson, "We never pay for options anymore. If an agent tries to hold us up for even a small amount of money, we tell them to take the script someplace else."

This is a Market in Hell, as far as writers are concerned, so until this situation changes, be prepared for the worst.

Understand I am talking about options here, not development money, which is what a studio will pay a writer for rewriting a purchased script. The "option" is the step before this part of the process, during which a producer tries to put together a package to sell to the studio, which then initiates further development of the script.

Between a Rock and a Hard Place

This atmosphere can mean difficult choices for a screenwriter. Let me share a personal example from August 1999.

A producer held an option for one of my screenplays that was up for renewal. By the contract, a $500 fee would extend the renewal six months. The producer, however, called my agent and said he wanted a free extension.

My agent advised that we should tell the producer "no deal". Pay up or shut up. This made perfect sense: a contract is a contract. I agreed, and my agent called the producer.

The producer was very upset. He called me personally.

He made the "real world" argument: if I didn't renew the option, I might find another producer to option it—but in today's market, that option would be free anyway, so I was not going to make any money by turning him down. Moreover, he was familiar with the script like no one else, had worked on rewrites with me for nine months. He loved the script and was its best salesman. Why go back to point zero at this late date?

I asked my agent what she thought. Shelve it, she said. I had exhausted my contacts the first time through, finally getting this option.

In other words, I had three choices: shelve the script; market it myself, for at best a free option; or let the producer run with it for another six months.

I finally chose the latter. It seemed to me this was the only alternative with a longshot attractive outcome. The producer was excited about the script, and he did know it as well as I did. Another persuasive fact was that our collaborative rewrite resulted in a better script. And yes, he had something to do with that.

This was not an easy decision. None of the options are what writers should be faced with. Unfortunately, I don't see the WGA doing anything to improve this new market climate.

But sometimes something good can happen from the leap of faith associated with a free option. One screenwriter shared this story on the Internet's screenwriting newsgroup (*misc.writing.screenplays*):

> A spec of ours that hadn't sold was noticed by a pair of young would-be producers, who asked us to give them a free (non-exclusive) option. They were nice, bright, and seemed to be go-getters. We let them run with it. They set up a negative pickup deal, the film got made, and the whole thing turned out to be a pretty good experience. (And brought us a nice hunk of change.)

Keeping the Faith

Talent, unfortunately, is often not enough, nor craft. You need something else: *ENDURANCE.*

William Faulkner had it right at the end of his Nobel Prize acceptance speech: we need to endure. In life. And in the screenwriting business.

The best way to endure is to keep busy, putting one foot before the other, daily, steadily—and trying to enjoy your work every step of the way.

Keep writing.

Keep marketing.

Exercises

1. Make a list of your screenwriting goals. Note whether you aspire to write screenplays full or part time; whether you aspire to make and/or produce films. What genres will you specialize in? Keep this list visible and regularly check it against your actual efforts.

2. Make a formal marketing plan, following the guidelines in this chapter. In particular, set aside a few hours each week when you will regularly market your work.

3. Become active in the Internet's screenwriting community. This community is constantly changing and growing, so you'll need to do some research to discover where you fit in. The newsgroup *misc. writing.screenplays* is a good place to begin. Consider starting your own screenwriting group, online or in your community if there are enough screenwriters.

16

BUILDING A SCREENWRITING CAREER

There are many ways to "be" a screenwriter—including not "being" one at all!

For most of my writing career I was a playwright who also wrote screenplays. I defined myself this way to keep sane: the screenwriting business would drive me nuts if my major ego and financial energy were devoted to it.

I grew up in Los Angeles, receiving my B.A. at UCLA, and no longer choose to live there. I knew this amounted to a serious professional disadvantage and adjusted my goals accordingly.

Defining myself primarily as a playwright rather than a screenwright lets me sleep well at night. Today I have refocused my writing on fiction, where I began. I sleep well at night. Still, however, I love the screenplay form and love movies so much I always seem to be working on a new screenplay.

Do you want to be a screenwriter? Make sure you understand what you are getting into. Richard Price puts it this way in *American Screenwriters:*

> "Understand the nature of the screenwriter, that he serves people. You're a service craft. If you want to feel good about yourself, consider yourself a craftsman. The most important thing in getting a job is not how well you write—because if they don't know you, they won't ask for you. For them to want you, you have to go in there with a great story."

As we've seen before, "the idea is king" and success begins with a great story concept.

Find Your World

Who are you? What do you want from screenwriting?

How you answer determines how you go about building your screenwriting career. There are other questions:

175

What are your goals? What kind of movies do you want to write and for what market (the studio system, the indies, or the small budgets)? Are you interested in rewriting or script doctor work? Will you write only screenplays—or will you be working in other genres, such as fiction, theater, poetry, or journalism? Do you want to be a full-time screenwriter or write as part of another career, such as teaching? Where do you want to be two years from now? Five? Ten?

You need to define your world as a screenwriter, a screenwright, in as much detail as you can.

Whatever screenwriting world you enter, you're going to have to face some unpleasant facts. You will often face putting a script into what is called "development hell," a collaborative process from which it may never emerge. Consider this observation from *FrameWork*, a history of screenwriting:

> In the eighties, the process of development became so complex that writers spent most of their time either taking meetings to pitch an idea or script or doing rewrites on their own or someone else's script. By the mid-eighties, the major companies combined were investing between thirty and fifty million dollars a year in the development process. Most of the scripts in development were not made.

Indeed, 9 out of 10 were not made.

A screenwriter must learn how to hustle. Again, from *FrameWork*: "Screenwriters have always had to hustle, but the more the process of screenwriting moves away from the family feeling of silent films or the organized procedures of the studio system, the more the screenwriters have had to learn how to manipulate the system, or, increasingly, the systems of filmmaking."

Screenwriting, in whatever world, is no "writer's paradise," certainly not the way we would define a novelist or poet, an artist with control and rhetorical responsibility. Writers are closer to hired hands in the film world and the closer your own world moves to the Hollywood mainstream, the more this is true.

Prioritize Your Energy

Once you know how screenwriting fits into your world, look at how you spend your time. Prioritize your energy so as much time as possible is spent reaching your goal, which I assume is to live fully in the world you've defined.

If you want screenwriting to be your life, however, if you want to work within the studio system and get assignments, you need to be where the action is, in Los Angeles. If you're not there already, you need to figure out how to get there and how to survive once you are. In contrast, a writer who is primarily a novelist and wants to write screenplays on the side has no reason to move to L.A.

These two writers would prioritize their energies differently. The former has a lot of "non-screenwriting craft" issues to deal with, while the latter can simply concentrate on learning how to craft a good screenplay. If the former has a degree in accounting, finding an accounting job in Los Angeles might be a high priority. Once there, the person can concentrate on changing careers.

Every case will be different, and only you can define your world and figure out the best way to reach your goals.

Your Movie Concept—Again ·

The more I learn about the business, the more I realize how much it's concept-driven. Indeed, it has been said that the only people who are writing spec scripts—that is to say, the only people who are writing before getting paid—are people outside the system. People in the system pitch concepts, not scripts. They don't begin to write until they have a deal.

Concepts are king. And good concepts are maddeningly difficult to create! Once you hear a good concept—an estranged father cross-dresses as a nanny in order to visit his children—it rings immediately true. We think, Why didn't I think of that? But coming up with these "natural" concepts is much harder than you think.

So I urge you to pay more attention to the very beginning of the process—the movie concept. Once you've learned the craft, it's tempting to jump in and exercise it with the first "good story" idea you get. But "good" isn't enough.

Be tough on yourself. Don't settle for just any "good" concept. Keep struggling and don't start writing until you've found that "great" concept. Of course, one person's "great" is not another's—you can't escape subjectivity.

At the same time, you need to move beyond writing stories that only interest you. Writer Kurt Wimmer puts it this way (quoted in *Big Deal*):

> "Most first-time, second-time, third-time and tenth-time writers have difficulty suppressing themselves and their screenplays and the stories they find interesting, as opposed to the stories they think are interesting and they think the entire movie-going public—and therefore the studios—would be interested in."

You'll know when a concept rings "true and great," the way the concept for *Mrs. Doubtfire* rings true and great with me. Hopefully, your taste will be in sync with Hollywood power brokers.

Or at least with one of them.

Your Movie Ideas

Continue adding to your notebook or file of movie concepts (notes and loglines). Review these periodically to see which still resonate with you. If you don't like them any more, discard them. Try to isolate concepts that ring "true and great" with you over time. These are the scripts to start working on.

You can look for concepts even as you're working on a script—and should be! In fact, I think you should always be writing down new ideas and concepts for future scripts. The working screenwright is always busy:

- Writing a new script
- Rewriting a previous script
- Marketing a finished script or scripts
- Creating new movie concepts

The working screenwright is always writing.

Find Opportunities

Digital technology makes moviemaking easier than ever—and where movies are being made, there are opportunities for screenwriters.

Look around you. Who is walking around with a digital video camera, making a movie? Maybe they need help. The more you know about how movies are made, the better your screenwriting will become.

Film schools offer opportunities. Not all budding filmmakers write their own scripts. Maybe they need a short script for a school project. Maybe you're the person to write it.

Should You Move to Los Angeles?

The short answer is yes. The long answer includes exceptions to the short answer.

You don't have to move to L.A. if:

- Screenwriting will not be your primary career.
- Quality of life is more important to you than success in Hollywood.
- You have other reasons to live elsewhere, such as raising a family.
- You have no interest in "taking meetings" or getting rewrite assignments.
- You can afford to fly to L.A. as often as it takes.

But if you want to work in the heart of the system, prepare to move to Los Angeles. You have two strikes against you if you don't.

The better news is you don't have to do this immediately. You need to learn the craft first, and you can do this anywhere.

When you consistently get producers interested in your screenwriting, you'd better start reading the handwriting on the wall. Living in L.A. is what most screenwriters have to do. I've had agents who were very much behind my work—until they learned that I would not relocate to Los Angeles.

However, the dissenting opinion may give distant screenwriters hope. According to Thom Taylor in *Big Deal*, living and working outside the mainstream offers advantages: "Modern technology has allowed writers to remain in their indigenous environments. And because Hollywood loves what's unattainable, being further from the center of heat can add to a screenwriter's fire."

Becoming a successful screenwriter is not easy, and success sometimes makes writers scarred and bitter (even if wealthy). Bruce Joel Rubin (*Ghost*) offers this advice (from *American Screenwriters*):

> "I feel very badly for people who get bitter and sour out here. It's so sad to watch it happen to sweet and juicy people. But it does. That's the sad part of Hollywood. It eats people up. And unless you can eat it up, you're going to have a problem. There's no guarantee on which way it's going to work. But if you can have something in life that's more important to you than writing movies, chances are you'll survive this better than if movies are your only source of nurturing."

Final Thoughts

We're at the end of this book and self-guided course. I wish I had something profound to say, but I don't.

Maybe I'll start where I began: I love screenwriting, and I hate screenwriting. I also have a dream.

My dream is that digital movies are going to be produced that will never see theatrical release. Instead they will be distributed through the World Wide Web, where customers will download them directly to their home entertainment screens.

In other words, digital filmmakers will have the option of becoming their own distributors by creating a website. If this happens, an extraordinary amount of independent artistic energy will be released.

I don't think the powers that be want this to happen because they know more than they let on. One thing they know is that the movie audience is smarter than they give it credit for. People want good stories about real people.

The Digital Revolution

An early consequence of the digital revolution is the movie *The Anniversary Party* (2001), cowritten and codirected by, and costarring the wonderful actress Jennifer Jason Leigh and shot entirely on video with the incredibly low budget of under 4 million dollars. The budget is particularly extraordinary when you hear that the movie features "high priced" stars like Gwyneth Paltrow and Kevin Kline, who obviously worked for a friend for peanuts.

What we have here is the "star" equivalent of the film student's low-budget movie. Many of the same constraints and story strategies apply. The entire story has one central location, the house where the anniversary party takes place. The story is character-driven, an ensemble piece. There are no special effects and less visual storytelling than is common in a Hollywood movie. The film, in fact, has a definite "stage play" feel.

The Anniversary Party is a play-like, character-driven ensemble story—with Hollywood stars in all the roles! Only digital technology makes this adventure possible. It will be interesting to see what other stars will use this revolution to turn from actor to writer/director.

It also will be interesting to see how audiences respond to this movie and others like it. If such films do well, it's a point for the kind of character-driven, slowly developing story that used to be the mainstay of theater but difficult to market to Hollywood. In other words, new story strategy options are being offered to mainstream audiences now. If audiences react positively, this might permanently affect how stories are told in Hollywood.

I think Hollywood is afraid of the level playing field that could result from movie distribution via the Web, bypassing the usual channels. I think great untapped audiences, starving for quality film entertainment, will be reached for the first time. Independent filmmakers and writers whose material would never reach a mass audience could finally make a decent living.

Consider retired people as an audience. They have lots of time on their hands, but they don't like to go out much because it's become so dangerous. Movies like *Cocoon* and *Driving Miss Daisy* fit this audience perfectly—but how many get made? How much time passes before the movies get shown on TV so the audience can see them at home?

Digital movies delivered weekly (or more frequently!) to home entertainment screens from the net would serve this audience perfectly. So we need 50 or 100 or 200 movies made every year for the senior citizen market.

Late in 2001, the PBS show *Frontline* focused on how Hollywood has changed in recent years, mostly in ways not encouraging to writers and others who favor non-formulaic storytelling. The good news, however, was about the possibilities of the digital revolution and its effects on the film industry, including screenwriters. The show was called "The Monster That Ate Hollywood" and I recommend it.

The digital revolution's possibilities are encouraging. This and the present tense of screenwriting, when the magic of a story consumes me, are what keep me going.

Find something that keeps you going.

There are other reasons to be optimistic. Jon Glickman thinks the future bodes well for screenwriters (quoted in *Big Deal*):

> "Writers are probably the most safe going into the next world because stories are always going to stay the same. You're always going to need to have a good story.... Whoever produces it may be different, the companies may change. But you're always going to need stories, and story construction has been the same since 600 B.C., or whenever. I don't see that aspect of the business changing. There's not going to be some new storytelling, so I think writers are the one constant."

At the 1999 WGA awards, *Taxi Driver* writer Paul Schrader accepted his first-ever screenwriting award and made these remarks (quoted in *Big Deal*):

> "Sooner or later, the kind of work I do will be acknowledged. It's nice to have it happen while you're still alive. But when you do this sort of thing, you have to believe in history and you have to believe in the ancestry of art. You have to believe that you're filing things in the archives. Maybe they will be appreciated in your lifetime and maybe they won't. It doesn't really matter."

Another award recipient at this ceremony, Frank Pierson, lamented the present state of the industry:

> "I'm really disturbed about two things today. One is that among the big audience pictures, which are being financed by the major studios, the range of subject matter is so narrow and is aimed at a particularly small and not especially demanding audience. That's an impoverishment of our intellectual and cultural life that I really, truly regret.

"The other thing, which I see with the people that I am teaching, is a matching impoverishment of the language of film that we share with an audience—a language we can use to push the envelope and expand an audience's ideas and feelings. Lamentably, that envelope has gotten very thin and shredded.

"Kids coming along tend to assume that they can automatically, intuitively write, direct and act, without ever having learned the language and the craft of those professions. For most of my students now, film history began with Steven Spielberg. Ironically, Steven himself was brought up studying the films of people who had a broad literary and liberal arts background—a deep understanding of the culture in which all this fits. And that's all missing now, or it tends to be skimmed over.

"So the only thing we can do is just beat the hell out of these kids and say, 'Listen, the films you're making are shit, and the stories you're telling are not worth hearing. They do not advance us at all in our knowledge of the human condition. Now, let's go back and talk about why they're that way and how we can make them better.'"

Are screenplays literature? Do they strive to reach such a high standard? In the history of film, they have been, first and foremost, entertainment. But there have been serious films, too, that aspire to the same narrative goals as literature.

You, the future generation of screenwriters, will determine what films become. I hope you have high standards. I hope you tell stories about real people, stories that matter.

I wish you well on your journey.

BIBLIOGRAPHY

Books
Joseph Campbell, *The Hero's Journey* (Harper & Row, 1990)
Tom Chiarella, *Writing Dialogue* (Story Press, 1998)
Anne Dean, *David Mamet: Language as Dramatic Action* (Fairleigh Dickinson University Press, 1990)
Michael B. Druxman, *The Art of Storytelling* (The Center Press, 1997)
Andre Dubus, *In the Bedroom* (Vintage, 2002)
John Gregory Dunne, *Monster: Living Off the Big Screen* (Random House, 1997)
Lajos Egri, *The Art of Dramatic Writing* (Simon & Schuster, 1977)
Syd Field, *Screenplay: the Foundations of Screenwriting* (Bantam, 1994)
William Froug, *Screenwriting Tricks of the Trade* (Silman-James, 1993)
William Goldman, *Adventures in the Screen Trade* (Warner Brothers, 1983)
Michael Hauge, *Writing Screenplays That Sell* (McGraw-Hill, 1980)
Lew Hunter, *Screenwriting 434* (A Perigee Book, 1993)
Christopher Keane, *How to Write a Selling Screenplay* (Broadway Books, 1998)
Robert Kosberg, *How to Sell Your Idea to Hollywood* (HarperPerennial, 1991)
Susan Kouguell, *The Savvy Screenwriter* (TL Hoell Books, 2000)
Jennifer Lerch, *500 Ways to Beat the Hollywood Script Reader* (Fireside, 1999)
David Morrell, *Lessons from a Lifetime of Writing* (Writer's Digest Books, 2001)
Linda Palmer, *How to Write It, How to Sell It* (St. Martin's Griffin, 1998)
John Roach & Mary Sweeney, *The Straight Story* (Hyperion, 1999)
Robin U. Russin and William Missouri Downs, *Screenplay: Writing the Picture* (Harcourt, 1999)
Karl Schanzer & Thomas Lee Wright, *American Screenwriters* (Avon Books, 1993)
Rick Schmidt, *Feature Filmmaking at Used Car Prices* (Penguin Books, 1995)
Sol Stein, *Stein on Writing* (St. Martin's Press, 1995)
Tom Stempel, *FrameWork: A History of Screenwriting in the American Film* (Continuum, 1988)
Linda Stuart, *Getting Your Script Through the Hollywood Maze* (Acrobat Books, 1993)
Kristin Thompson, *Storytelling in the New Hollywood: Understanding Classical Narrative Technique* (Harvard University Press, 1999)
David Trottier, *The Screenwriter's Bible* (Silman-James Press, 1995)
Chris Vogel, *The Writer's Journey* (Michael Wiese, 1992)
Richard Walter, *Screenwriting* (A Plume Book, 1988)
Richard Walter, *The Whole Picture* (Penguin, 1997)
Rich Whiteside, *The Screenwriting Life: the Dream, the Job, and the Reality* (Berkley Boulevard Books, 1998)
Jurgen Wolff and Kerry Cox, *Top Secrets: Screenwriting* (Lone Eagle Publishing Co., 1993)
Justin Wyatt, *High Concept: Movies and Marketing in Hollywood* (Texas Film Studies, 1995)

Screenplays
Sherman Alexie, *Smoke Signals* (Hyperion, 1998)
Paul Thomas Anderson, *Magnolia* (Newmarket Press, 2000)
Alan Ball, *American Beauty* (Newmarket Press, 1999)

Nora Ephron, *When Harry Met Sally* (Knopf, 1997)
Rob Festinger and Todd Field, *In the Bedroom* (Hyperion, 2002)
David Mamet, *House of Games* (Grove Weidenfeld, 1987)
Elaine May, *The Birdcage* (Newmarket Press, 1997)
Marc Norman and Tom Stoppard, *Shakespeare in Love* (Hyperion, 1998)
Thom Taylor, *The Big Deal* (William Morrow, 1999)
Billy Bob Thornton, *Sling Blade* (Hyperion, 1996)

Internet
Terry Rossio, "A Foot in the Door," http://www.wordplayer.com/columns/wp01.A.Foot.in.the.Door.html
David Trottier's column, "Breaking In," http://hollywoodnet.com/Trottier/idea.html
Terry Rossio, "Beachcombing," http://www.wordplayer.com/columns/wp03.Beachcombing.html
Interview with Christopher McQuarrie, http://www.teleport.com/~cdeemer/interview-cmq.html
Aristotle's Poetics, Book VII, translated by S. H. Butcher, http://classics.mit.edu//Aristotle/poetics.7.vii.html
Screenwright: The Craft of Screenwriting, http://www.screenwright.com
Indiezine, http://telluridemm.com/indizine.html
Richard Toscan's Playwriting Seminars, http://www.vcu.edu/artweb/playwriting/
The Fiction Writers' Home Page and the Jarvis Method, http://www.writerspage.com
Essays on the Craft of Dramatic Writing by Bill Johnson, http://www.teleport.com/~bjscript/index.htm
Understanding What a Story Is by Bill Johnson, http://www.teleport.com/~bjscript/wstoryis.htm
Understanding the Process of Storytelling by Bill Johnson, http://www.teleport.com/~bjscript/wprocess.htm
Foundation Principles of Storytelling by Bill Johnson, http://www.teleport.com/~bjscript/wfound.htm
The Screenwriters Home Page by Brad Mirman, http://home.earthlink.net/~scribbler/
Drew's Scripts-O-Rama, http://www.script-o-rama.com
2-Goal, 9-Act Structure Page, http://www.dsiegel.com/film/
Wordplay, "How Do You Get An Agent?" by Dan Petrie, Jr., http://www.wordplayer.com/pros/pr04a.Petrie.Dan.Jr.html

Useful screenwriting websites
Writers Guild of America, http://www.wga.org. Register scripts online.
Coming Attractions by Corona, http://corona.bc.ca/films/filmlistings.html. Database of films in various stages of production.
Done Deal, http://www.scriptsales.com/. Database of recent script sales.
Hollywood Lit Sales, http://www.hollywoodlitsales.com/. Sales database plus free online pitching.
Screenwriters Utopia, http://www.screenwritersutopia.com. One of the first screenwriting websites. Charles Deemer publishes a monthly screenwriting column here.
Screenwriting Basics, http://www.geocities.com/cdeemer/Screen.htm. Maintained by Charles Deemer.

APPENDICES

APPENDIX 1

Examples of Movie Story Structure

1940s movies:

- *Citizen Kane*
- *Bambi*
- *It's a Wonderful Life*

1950s movies:

- *High Noon*
- *The Caine Mutiny*

1960s movies:

- *The Hustler*
- *The Graduate*

1970s movies:

- *Chinatown*
- *American Graffiti*
- *Carrie*
- *Taxi Driver*

1980s movies:

- *Atlantic City*
- *Body Heat*
- *E.T.*

- *My Dinner With Andre*

1990s movies:

- *Thelma and Louise*
- *Shakespeare in Love*
- *The Sixth Sense*
- *Independence Day*

2000s movies:

- *A Beautiful Mind*
- *Monster's Ball*
- *My Big Fat Greek Wedding*
- *O Brother Where Art Thou?*
- *Traffic*
- *Far From Heaven*
- *Memento*
- *About Schmidt*
- *Adaptation*
- *The Hours*

1940s movies

Citizen Kane
written by Herman J. Mankiewicz and Orson Welles

Citizen Kane *is widely considered to be the best American movie ever made. Far ahead of its time in nonlinear storytelling techniques and cinematography effects, today it is a reminder of how even daring innovation of its time still honors the 3-act paradigm. The classic foundation— beginning, middle, end storytelling— is firmly in place in this masterpiece.*

STRUCTURAL ANALYSIS

Hook (0-2 min.) A "No Trespassing" sign immediately grabs our attention. We enter an incredible mansion, a palace, where the lips of a man say his dying words, "Rosebud..."

Complication (5-13 min.) A newsreel (the use of which was innovative) gives us a capsule biography of Charles Foster Kane, the man who just died wealthy, controversial, in the end lonely.

Call to Action (13 min.) The reporters putting together the "obituary newsreel" are missing a part of the puzzle, however. What does the dying word "Rosebud" mean? A reporter is assigned to find out.

Act One Plot Point (23, 31 min.) Now two narrative lines develop side by side: the reporter's quest to find the meaning of "Rosebud" and the deeper biography of Kane that he learns along the way. In the latter, Kane inherits great wealth as a young man (after being shipped away as a child by his mother, who wanted to protect him from an abusive father) but turns everything down except a struggling newspaper: he thinks it would be fun to run a newspaper (23 min.) The reporter is told that it wasn't money that Kane wanted, and that to learn about the real Kane he must go talk to his oldest friend.

Midpoint Plot Point (56-60 min.) Unhappily married, Kane meets a young woman who likes him even though she has no idea how rich and famous he is. He begins an affair with her, which he continues even after entering the race for governor. Later he will choose the other woman over his wife (69 min.), even as it destroys his political career.

Act Two Plot Point (104-6 min.) Kane builds an opera house for "the other woman" who becomes his wife. She's a terrible singer, and when she attempts suicide after his continued bullying about her doomed career (96 min.), he retreats with her into the reclusive life of the palace. She finally can't stand it any longer and leaves him (104-6 min.).

Climax and Resolution (114-7 min.) The reporter never learns what "Rosebud" means. As Kane's possessions are burned, his childhood sled is thrown into the fire, the sled named Rosebud. All his life, Kane longed for the simple but momentary happiness of his childhood before he was sent away.

NOTES

Citizen Kane is both a mystery, a puzzle—who or what was Rosebud?— and the biography of an extraordinary man. The device of the newsreel reporter searching for clues permits the biography to unwind slowly, keeping our interest, and the biography also follows the classic structure of beginning, middle, end storytelling. For all its innovation, this movie retains the oldest foundation of them all.

Bambi
written by Chuck Couch et. al.

Bambi is rich with rewards for those who will study its dramatic structure. At just over an hour in length, the Disney classic lends itself to close study in half the time it takes to study features. Yet the traditional 3-act paradigm is very much at work here, which is further testimony to its importance in all storytelling in our culture.

STRUCTURAL ANALYSIS

Hook (2 min.) Birds fly through the forest with an urgent message: "Wake up, wake up! It happened. The new prince is born." The new prince is Bambi.

Complication (5 min.) After all the forest animals rush to see the newly born Bambi, we see a magnificent stag high on a ridge overlooking the forest. We don't yet know the significance of this—but will soon enough. We know the stag will play an important role in our story.

Call to Action (7-10 min.) Bambi takes his first steps of discovery into the forest, learning to walk, learning to talk.

Act One Plot Point (25-7 min.) Bambi follows a rush of bucks and meets, eyeball-to-eyeball, the great stag who is "the Great Prince of the Forest." Bambi also learns that the forest is not Eden: first, when his mother warns him of danger in the unprotected meadow (17-18 min.), later when fear and hiding happen after "man was in the forest" (28-9 min.).

Midpoint Plot Point (38-40 min.) Hunters kill Bambi's mother. "Come, my son," says the great stag.

Act Two Plot Point (55-60 min.) Hunters cause a fire in the forest, and Bambi is separated from Faline, his lady deer, finally fighting off dogs to save her. But he is injured and only the admonitions of the great stag,

"Get up!" gives Bambi the energy to escape with other forest animals to an island, where he is reunited with Faline.

Climax and Resolution (64-5 min.) Faline has Bambi's two children, and on the ridge overlooking the forest, Bambi replaces the stag as the Great Prince.

NOTES

Bambi draws some memorable minor characters (Flower, Thumper) and reminds us how important they can be to a story. We need to give our human characters all the individuality that these animal characters have.

"American movies are about what happens next," wrote Richard Toscan, and *Bambi* is filled with twists and turns throughout its hour, providing an excellent model for suspenseful narrative. Pacing is relieved with musical numbers, which replace the "big sequences" of feature films, but these are not overdone, i.e., this is not a musical. *Bambi*, in fact, is a traditional coming-of-age love story. Study it carefully.

It's a Wonderful Life
written by Frances Goodrich, Albert Hackett, and Frank Capra

It's a Wonderful Life is a classic movie, of course, but also a very interesting one to study for its innovative use of the 3-act paradigm and its ability to maintain interest with smaller high-quality scenes.

STRUCTURAL ANALYSIS

Hook (0-3 min.) Everyone in Bedford Falls is praying for George Bailey. An angel, Clarence, will be sent down to answer their prayers—and also to earn his wings.

Complication (28 min.) After Clarence gets a background course on George (4-28 min.), the adult George is ready to go off on an exotic trip when his father has a stroke, forcing him to stay home. George wants nothing more than to leave Bedford Falls.

Call to Action (34 min.) George buries his father. The mean-spirited Potter is about to take over Bailey Building and Loan when the board votes him down on the condition that George stay and run the company. Although he's about to leave for college, George agrees in order to save his father's company.

Act One Plot Point (52-8 min.) About to leave on his honeymoon with Mary, George sees a run on the bank. Mary offers the honeymoon money, and they save the day and keep in business.

Midpoint Plot Point (80 min.) Uncle Billy loses an $8000 deposit on Christmas Eve, with a bank inspector at the office. Unless they replace it, the company will go bankrupt.

Act Two Plot Point (104 min.) Clarence jumps into the river so the distraught George will save him, rather than jumping himself. George wishes he had never been born, and Clarence grants the wish.

Climax and Resolution (121 min.) Seeing how different Bedford Falls and Mary and others he has touched would have been without him, George prays to live again, to have everything return to normal. The many people George has helped chip in to save his company. A man is as rich as the friends he has.

NOTES

It's a Wonderful Life pushes its major dramatic beats back about 24 minutes for the background flashback. This works because the flashback itself is filled with entertaining scenes—and because the initial hook is strong and unusual. Take away this "real time" and the components fall in more traditional order: complication at 4 min., call at 10 min., PPI at 28-34 min., midpoint at 56 min., and PPII at 80 min.

The flashback isn't over till the end of Act Two, when the story time at the beginning of the movie is reached. Act Three, then, is mainly George learning what the world would be like without him: Bedford Falls would be named Pottersville, a town full of bars; the druggist he saved from catastrophe would be an ex-con and rummy; his house would be abandoned, never renovated; his uncle would be in an insane asylum; his little brother would have died at 9, because George never rescued him, and therefore all the men the brother saved in the war would also have died; and his wife Mary would be an old-maid librarian.

This is a difficult structure that in less skilled hands would have been disastrous but it works beautifully here because interest in the movie never wanes and because the focus—Clarence's charge to save George—is never far from our attention.

1950s movies

High Noon
written by Carl Foreman

High Noon *is a classic western and psychological drama about a man who refuses to run from danger and duty.*

STRUCTURAL ANALYSIS

Hook (0-6 min.) The outlaw Ben Miller and friends are in town. For what?

Complication (9 min.) Brother outlaw Frank Miller has been paroled—and is due on the noon train. And this on the day of the sheriff's wedding and retirement.

Call to Action (12 min.) Will Kane, the sheriff, tries to leave town with his bride but can't. He's the one who sent Miller to prison. Moreover, he had an affair with his girl. He decides he must stay or face running from Miller for the rest of his life.

Act One Plot Point (33-8 min.) Kane tries to raise deputy support—and gets only one volunteer, who expects there to be many others. He is going to have to do this alone.

Midpoint Plot Point (51-4 min.) Kane's isolation is deepened as everyone from a friend and supporter to his mentor advises him to leave town before noon, when Miller will arrive. Kane still won't go.

Act Two Plot Point (70-3 min.) The train arrives. The gunfight begins: Kane against four outlaws.

Climax and Resolution (82-4 min.) At the last minute his wife stays and shoots one of the outlaws in the back. When she is taken hostage by Frank Miller, the last outlaw left, she gets away long enough for Kane to kill him. He throws down his badge in disgust as the cowardly townsfolk gather, and he and his wife leave for good.

NOTES

High Noon has a literal ticking clock through most of the movie, tension building as noon approaches. Dialogue here is crisp and focused, a good deal of the story being told visually. There are many layers of psychological complication that add to the density of the story: the wife's being a Quaker, Kane's relationship with Miller's old girl, the deputy who is jealous of him (and the new lover for the girl), the excuses made by everyone not to help him. This is more psychological drama than traditional western.

The Caine Mutiny
written by Stanley Roberts

The Caine Mutiny is a war drama about an eccentric C.O. whose men decide to "over-throw" and the courts-martial that results. Perfect 3-act structure.

STRUCTURAL ANALYSIS
<u>Hook</u> (1 min.) In the heat of WWII, the Navy sends "90 day wonders" (new officers) to war. One is our protagonist.
<u>Complication</u> (10 min.) But our protagonist is assigned to a tub, the *Caine*, in the "junkyard Navy."
<u>Call to Action</u> (16 min.) Nonetheless, our protagonist turns down an opportunity to transfer and remains on the *Caine*.
<u>Act One Plot Point</u> (28-31 min.) A new C.O. will make the *Caine* the best ship in the Navy, and our protagonist is appointed to be Morale Officer.
<u>Midpoint Plot Point</u> (58-9 min.) Is the new C.O. crazy? The junior officers, including the protagonist, wonder. A diary is kept on his eccentric behavior.
<u>Act Two Plot Point</u> (83-86 min.) Backed by the protagonist, the Executive Officer relieves the C.O. from duty during a life-threatening storm. The protagonist loses his fiancée, who breaks up with him.
<u>Climax and Resolution</u> (112-5 min.) During the trial, the C.O. betrays himself—he is mad. The protagonist gets his girl back and they marry.

1960s movies

The Hustler
written by Sydney Carroll and Robert Rosen

The Hustler, a classic poolroom drama, is a hero's journey story, about a lowlife sort who through personal tragedy learns how to care about people.

STRUCTURAL ANALYSIS
<u>Hook</u> (3-5 min.) Fast Eddie and his partner hustle unsuspecting pool players in a small-town pool hall.
<u>Complication</u> (11 min.) Fast Eddie wants to play Minnesota Fats, the best pool player in the game. He wants to win ten grand in a single night. He is ambitious and cocky.

Call to Action (15 min.) Fast Eddie challenges Fats to play at $200 a game. The game begins.

Act One Plot Point (35 min.) Eddie blows a big lead to lose a marathon match to a refreshed Fats. Then he falls down drunk. Later he meets a woman at a bus station (39 min.) and will move in with her (55 min.).

Midpoint Plot Point (74, 79 min.) Eddie turns down his old partner. Later he gets caught hustling and has his thumbs broken.

Act Two Plot Point (115 min.) Back in form, Eddie is winning—but he loses Sarah, who sees him being used. She leaves him. When Eddie goes looking for her, he finds her dead (121 min.).

Climax and Resolution (124, 130-3 min.) Eddie plays a $300 game rematch with Fats and wins. He refuses to pay up an old debt and gets banned from pool halls but is ready to walk away from the hustler's life. He feels guilty about Sarah; he loved her.

NOTES

The Hustler has one of the best examples in film of pure visual storytelling. After Eddie hustles Sarah at the bus station, she initially rejects him at her apartment ("you're too hungry"). Later, however, she returns to find him again drinking coffee in the bus station (52 min.). Beginning writers would fill this scene with dialogue, probably poor dialogue at that. Here there is no dialogue at all. Their eyes meet. Eddie gets up and walks to her. They turn and silently leave, arm in arm. It's an emotionally powerful moment, two loners giving in to one another, the catalyst for Eddie's transformation, and it's all communicated without a single line of dialogue.

The Graduate
written by Buck Henry and Calder Willingham

The Graduate is a comedy that is filled with plot twists and extended sequences. It's a wonderful movie to study for three-act structure form and for the various paradigms that spin off of it. It also is one of the more interesting movies to compare with the "final draft" of the screenplay to see how the process of tightening the story doesn't stop with finishing the script but continues into the editing room.

STRUCTURAL ANALYSIS

The Hook (2 min.) Father asks Ben, "What's the matter?" Ben's concerns about his future.

Complication (7 min.) Mrs. Robinson to Ben, "Take me home."

Call to Action (14 min.) Mrs. Robinson undresses, says to Ben, "I'm available to you. Give me a call."

Act One Plot Point: (23-37 min.) Ben calls Mrs. Robinson, gets room, ends up staying with her. Starts the affair.

Midpoint Plot Point: (45-69 min.) First fight, Ben promises Mrs. Robinson not to take out her daughter, Elaine, but his parents put him up to it. Ben likes Elaine and tells her about the affair with her mother. Elaine: "Get out!" Ben loses both Mrs. Robinson and Elaine. Then he announces he plans to marry Elaine.

Act Two Plot Point: (92 min.) Mr. Robinson learns about the affair, bans Ben from seeing Elaine just after he has successfully wooed her back. All appears lost.

Climax and Resolution (103 min.) Ben rescues Elaine from church right after she is married. They take the bus into the sunset.

NOTES

Big Sequences

One of the wonderful things about the structure of *The Graduate* is that several of the big sequences lead directly to plot points. Here are some major moments:

Ben's swimming pool scuba diver's birthday present. (21 min.) Ben starting affair with Mrs. Robinson, leading to Act I plot point. (23 min.) Ben's comic courtship of Elaine in Berkeley. (73 min.) Ben learning of and trying to stop Elaine's wedding, leading to the resolution. (97 min.)

Some other lessons from *The Graduate*:

The screenwriter as architect: Someone once said that a screenplay is not a work of art but the invitation to the collaboration of a work of art. The screenwriter begins the process by putting down the dramatic structure of a story. But look at this movie and consider how important the music by Simon and Garfunkel is in the entire effect of the film. There is no mention of this in the script. The screenwriter, by nature, is a collaborator and a team player, closer to the architect than to the novelist or poet.

Visual storytelling: Motion pictures = pictures in motion: to tell a story with pictures is the task of the screenwriter. Here there are long wonderful sequences without dialogue, as when Ben goes to Berkeley to find, and then to stalk, and then to woo, Elaine.

The ticking clock (again): If you can get the sense of a ticking clock into your third act, you have done something that will establish the growing jeopardy and tension at the climax of your story. Here it is Ben racing against time to find Elaine before she is married. And even when he fails, standing up behind the glass in the church, wailing and pounding the window—when Elaine sees him, she is able to yell, "Ben!" and bring the movie to its happy ending.

1970s movies

Chinatown
written by Robert Towne

Robert Towne's Chinatown *is one of those scripts that has won the Syd Field Paradigm Perfect Screenplay Award and as a result probably has been studied in screenwriting classes more often than any other script. But this both flatters and insults the three-act paradigm.*

It flatters it because it implies that all one has to do is write a "paradigm perfect" script and success is guaranteed. Nothing could be farther from the truth—which is that many terrible scripts, horrendous scripts, also follow the three-act paradigm.

The popularity of Chinatown *as an object for study insults the paradigm by suggesting that it is some kind of special "honor" to be structured in three acts.*

The three-act paradigm (beginning-middle-end) is nothing less than the grammar of storytelling in this culture. You need to adhere to it because the paradigm defines the rules for dramatic communication. But this means only that you are now allowed to play the game, not that you automatically are going to play it well.

A powerful screenplay is a gestalt of many things, with structure being the most fundamental and necessary, but also something that good and bad movies alike can share. Just because you know the language doesn't mean that you're not going to speak gibberish.

STRUCTURAL ANALYSIS

<u>The Hook</u> (0 min.) We start off with a bang, from the first frame. A man is groaning as we see photos of lovemaking. Adultery has been captured on film, taken by the detective who is our hero, Jake, and the groans belong to the cheating woman's husband. We are in the thick of a story from the get-go—even though this is not the story that is the focus of the film. But we won't know the movie we've actually seen till the end, which is one of the strengths of this gripping tale.

<u>Complication</u> (17 min.) Jake is hired by a Mrs. Mulray to follow her husband, and what Jake learns—that Mr. Mulray, head of LA's water and power department, is having an affair—makes the paper. Then the real Mrs.

Mulray shows up, ready to sue Jake. She never hired him—and in fact is not the woman who hired Jake under the pretense of being Mrs. Mulray.

Call to Action (27 min.) Jake turns up many fishy things linking Mulray and LA's water issue. Mrs. Mulray is willing to drop the suit but Jake won't let this case go. He needs to know who set him up and why. It's a matter of professional pride.

Act One Plot Point: (31 min.) Mr. Mulray turns up dead, a victim of drowning.

Midpoint Plot Point: (64 min., 82 min.) There are two midpoints, it seems to me—a "professional" one regarding the plot at hand but also a "personal" one which gets Jake involved in his investigation at a personal level: Professional (64 min.): Jake gets hired by Mrs. Mulray's father to find the girl that Mulray was having an affair with; Personal (82 min.): Jake becomes romantically involved with Mrs. Mulray.

Act Two Plot Point: (109 min.) Mrs. Mulray reveals that "the other woman" is both her sister and her daughter—the child she had by her father.

Climax and Resolution (127 min.) Trying to help Mrs. Mulray escape with her daughter, Jake only manages to get her killed—just like what happened to him before in Chinatown when he got too personally involved.

NOTES

Big Sequences

Big sequences usually have great visual interest, as is the case here.

Sheep are driven into a city meeting as farmers protest the LA drought. (5 min.) Jake discovers a great flood of water turned loose into a dry river bank, almost getting swept away by the water—and gets his nose sliced when he is found out. (38 min.) A car chase through an orange grove. (68 min.)

Other points from *Chinatown*:

Visual storytelling: Since Jake is a detective whose job in part is tailing people, a lot of no-dialogue suspenseful sequences are possible here. Always look for ways to tell your story visually without words. Don't forget that "moving pictures" are one of your basic tools.

Subterfuge: This movie is filled with brilliant false leads. Towne manages to give us "facts" important to the story throughout—but also manages to present them the first time in a context that leads us, along with Jake, to wrong conclusions about them: Jake finds Mrs. Mulray keeping "Mulray's woman" in a house—and later learns it is her daughter/sister she is hiding from her father. Jake finds glasses in the pond, believing they belong to Mulray and are proof he was murdered at home. But they belong to the killer, Mrs. Mulray's father. Jake thinks Mrs. Mulray is fleeing because she is guilty of murdering her husband, not because she is a victim of abuse trying to protect her daughter from her father.

Efficient scene design: Almost all beginning screenwriters are very inefficient in their scene design, starting scenes too early and ending them too late. The secret is to begin in the middle of an action and to get out as soon as the scene has done its job. Study the scene transitions carefully in this movie. Notice how the scene cut is from Jake's bleeding nose directly to Jake wrapped in bandages. An amateur would take us to the hospital, which has nothing to do with the story. Don't give us anything in a scene that doesn't have a function. Sometimes here we don't know why we are getting information. For example, when we learn that Mrs. Mulray's maiden name was Cross. The information seems to come out of nowhere. But only a few minutes later we learn that Cross and Mulray owned the water and power company privately as partners before it became public. The Mulray-Cross stories become intertwined, though we have no way of knowing the true horror of this combination.

Visual exposition: Exposition—telling the audience facts it needs to know to understand the story—is always a challenge to a writer. You can do this subtly and visually, as here when Jake finds a political flier on a car with the headline, "LA Dying of Thirst." This is far better than Jake or someone saying, "Gee, it sure is quite a drought we've been having."

Who's the antagonist?: The real antagonist in this story is Mrs. Mulray's father—but we don't learn this till the last act. Who carries the burden of the antagonist until then? The mystery does. Jake's quest is to find out who the antagonist really is, and we get to go along for the ride.

Where's the happy ending?: Probably 99% of successful Hollywood movies have a happy ending. *Chinatown* ends with Mrs. Mulray, a victim of abuse, dead and the abuser, her father, walking off into the sunset with his daughter/granddaughter. Talk about the bad guys winning! It works here because we are in the film noir genre, the dark cynical form of mystery where bad guys get to win (*Body Heat* is another example), and because the ride itself is so suspenseful and gripping that we enjoy this for its own sake. But if you are going to write a script where the antagonist wins, you had better be damn good at it.

American Graffiti
written by George Lucas and Gloria Katz & Willard Huyck

American Graffiti has become a classic. The story follows four teenagers on a night in 1964, as two of them prepare to leave for college the next day.

STRUCTURAL ANALYSIS

Hook (1 min.) Curt and Steve are leaving for college the next day. This is their last night in town.

Complication (2 min.) But Curt, despite winning the Moose Lodge Scholarship, has decided not to leave town after all.

Call to Action (12 min.) "I saw a goddess," Curt says, a blonde driving a white T-bird, and the vision answers his earlier question, "Where's the dazzling beauty I've been waiting for?" He will find her.

Act One Plot Point (40-3 min.) Seeing the white T-bird again, Curt becomes obsessed with meeting the mystery woman.

Midpoint Plot Point (54 min.) For sitting on a stranger's car, Curt is taken "hostage" by some gang members.

Act Two Plot Point (97 min.) After being released by the gang, Curt takes a record request to the local radio station, where the DJ says he just plays tapes, that Wolfman is on tape. It looks like his radio message to the blonde won't happen that night.

Climax and Resolution (101-6 min.) But the DJ is Wolfman and makes the dedication. Curt has a brief phone conversation with his goddess at a phone booth. He decides to go off to college after all.

NOTES

American Graffiti is an ensemble story, with each of the four characters having fully developed story lines. Steve, for example, decides not to leave for college and to stay with his high-school girlfriend instead. In the credits, Richard Dreyfus (who plays Curt) gets top billing and his story also presents the central issue of the story: should he leave his small town to move into the world at large by going off to college? His character arc moves his decision from "no" to "yes."

Carrie
written by Lawrence D. Cohen

Carrie, based on a Stephen King novel, is a story that combines the chills of a horror story with the sensitivity of its theme, the revenge of a likeable teenage girl on the brink of her womanhood.

STRUCTURAL ANALYSIS

<u>Hook</u> (1 min.) Carrie is ostracized in a volleyball game at school.

<u>Complication</u> (3-4 min.) Carrie bleeds in the shower at school—her first period. She has no idea what has happened, her mother being a religious kook. She is teased to tears.

<u>Call to Action</u> (26 min.) Learning she has a strange power to move objects (9, 17 min.), Carrie studies about the occult in the library.

<u>Act One Plot Point</u> (36-7 min.) A teacher helps Carrie create a better self-image for herself. A popular boy wants to take her to the prom.

<u>Midpoint Plot Point</u> (47 min.) Carrie stands up to her mother and will go to the prom.

<u>Act Two Plot Point</u> (74 min.) Carrie is led into a cruel trap—falsely elected prom queen in order to be dunked on stage with an overhead bucket of blood.

<u>Climax and Resolution</u> (76-89 min.) Carrie turns loose her powers, burning down the school and killing her mother before the mother stabs her. But Carrie then perishes in the collapse of her home.

NOTES

Carrie uses the suspenseful device of letting us, the audience, know what Carrie doesn't know. We see the bucket of blood set up and in place, we know what is bound to happen—and the suspense is waiting for it.

We care for Carrie, which makes this movie more than a genre piece. She is real and her troubled background is real—and when she turns havoc loose upon the world, we understand why she is doing it.

Taxi Driver
written by Paul Schrader

Taxi Driver is a dark drama about a man who goes over the edge and in so doing, becomes an unlikely hero.

STRUCTURAL ANALYSIS

<u>Hook</u> (1-3 min.) An insomniac, Travis, talks himself into a job driving a cab. He is a haunting figure of a man. This is a character hook.

<u>Complication</u> (8 min.) Travis passes a woman on the street, who walks into the political campaign headquarters where she works. He sees her as an angel in the sordid mess all around him.

<u>Call to Action</u> (18 min.) Travis gets up nerve to barge into the campaign headquarters, meet the woman (Betsy) and talk himself into a date.

<u>Act One Plot Point</u> (33-6 min.) He makes the mistake of taking Betsy to a porno movie. She leaves in a huff and refuses to go out with him again.

<u>Midpoint Plot Point</u> (53-6 min.) Travis rises out of funk and depression after losing Betsy to prepare for war. He buys weapons, builds contraptions that hide them on his body, and works himself into great physical shape. He clearly is preparing for something.

<u>Act Two Plot Point</u> (95-7 min.) But his attempt to assassinate the senator for whom Betsy works fails when he is spotted. Instead he goes on a rampage against the pimp of an underage prostitute he has befriended, killing him and ending up in a shootout at the rooming house the young prostitute works out of, getting severely wounded himself.

<u>Climax and Resolution</u> (105-7 min.) Travis becomes a hero in the press and to the young prostitute's parents, who reunite with her and get her back in school. When Betsy climbs into his cab, making overtures that she might want to see him again, he drives off before she can pay her fare.

NOTES

This is an intense study of a troubled man, and there are very few moments when Travis is not in the focus of a scene. The antagonist here is the dreariness and decay of the urban center, the "scum" his taxi drives through each night. Has Travis made some peace with the world and himself after this strange journey to becoming a hero? The film leaves the answer ambiguous.

1980s movies

Atlantic City
written by John Guare

Atlantic City is a beautifully crafted script written by one of the best playwrights in the U.S. Few scripts so tightly weave the interplay of main and subplots, the latter informing the former. There's not a wasted beat in this fine film.

STRUCTURAL ANALYSIS

<u>Hook</u> (1-2 min.) The movie opens with a "soft hook," the image of the elderly Lou spying on his neighbor Sally as she washes her breasts with lemon juice (to remove the smell of fish from her work at a restaurant). The quick cut is to a story driving a subplot, Dave (Sally's husband, who ran off with her sister Crissie and has gotten her pregnant) picking up drugs dropped off at a phone booth just a step ahead of their intended recipient.

<u>Complication</u> (5 min.) Dave and Crissie come to Atlantic City, looking up Sally. She is furious to see them.

<u>Call to Action</u> (22 min.) Lou, who runs numbers and cares for Grace, a woman as old as he is, likes to pretend he's a big shot. He intercedes on Dave's behalf when Dave asks to use the phone in a bar. Dave befriends Lou by flattering him, in order to get the use of his apartment to prepare the drugs for sale on the street. Lou's kindness, then, thrusts him into the drug subplot that will drive the story.

<u>Act One Plot Point</u> (40-2 min.) While Lou helps out Dave by dropping off drugs (for $100), Dave is tracked down and killed. Now Lou is left with $4000 and the rest of the drugs.

<u>Midpoint Plot Point</u> (68 min.) The drug dealers rough up Sally, trying to get their drugs and money back, and Lou can't protect her. He has just made love to her—but he can't protect her. He feels defeated.

<u>Act Two Plot Point</u> (83-4 min.) The next time the dealers track them down, now aware that it is Lou with the drugs, Lou shoots them. He and Sally escape, Lou finally feeling like a big shot, the famous criminal he has always strived to be.

<u>Climax and Resolution</u> (94, 98 min.) Lou lets Sally escape with the money. He has set aside a small bit of the drugs, and at film's end he watches as Grace makes the delivery and collects the money. They walk off arm-in-arm, as happy as in the good old days.

NOTES

Atlantic City is about a man trying to recapture and glorify his past against changing times. Everywhere are images of the rebirth of Atlantic City as buildings are leveled to put up a casino, and as Lou loses numbers customers to those doing better playing slots.

Lou is a wonderful character, and his personal arc works in counterpoint to the arc of the story. He is at his low point at the midpoint. At the end of Act Two, when he puts himself in greatest jeopardy by murdering the two drug dealers, he feels on top of the world. This is a wonderful and skillfully executed variation of the usual arc that finds the protagonist at his lowest point going into Act Three. Lou ends up doing something noble, letting Sally get away with the money to begin her new life, and the movie ends before we see what consequences may await him—he has his moment of glory, a big shot bad guy at last, and we leave him proud and grinning.

Body Heat
written by Lawrence Kasdan

Body Heat is film noir at its best, a dark mystery about how a femme fatale cleverly gets an incompetent lawyer to murder her husband—and then take the rap for it.

STRUCTURAL ANALYSIS

<u>Hook</u> (6 min.) On a hot, humid night at Miranda Beach in Florida, Ned follows Matty and makes a move on her. We've already seen him with one woman in the opening scene. Will he score again?

<u>Complication</u> (10 min.) But when he returns from the men's room, she is gone.

<u>Call to Action</u> (11 min.) Ned learns she was from the upper-end Pinehaven—and sure enough, later he finds her in a bar there. He has gone out of his way to track her down—and boy, will he regret it.

<u>Act One Plot Point</u> (31 min., 44 min.) Ned and Matty start a passionate, highly erotic love affair. But her husband is in the way. "I wish he'd die," she tells him (31 min.). Ned tells her later that they will kill him themselves (44 min.).

<u>Midpoint Plot Point</u> (67 min.) Matty wants Ned to change her husband's will but he refuses. She'll get enough inheritance as it is. But after the murder, Ned is called in about an error in the new will he supposedly wrote for Matty's husband—and the invalid will means Matty gets everything after all. She forged the new will as written by Ned.

Act Two Plot Point (88-90 min.) Ned gets other clues that someone may be setting him up. On the night of the murder, someone phoned him repeatedly and he didn't answer. So much for an alibi. And the husband's glasses are missing. Later (90 min.) Ned learns that meeting Matty was not accidental—he was suggested to her by another lawyer, and she knows about earlier incompetence in his will writing. Is she setting him up? Apparently so.

Climax and Resolution (97-108 min.) Matty fakes her own death in an explosion meant for Ned—and Ned is jailed, taking the rap for it all. But in jail he guesses that she's still alive. As indeed she is, spending her inheritance at a beach resort with a new lover.

NOTES

Body Heat is worth careful study for the tightness of its clues and the subtle suspense that gets built along the ride. Scenes also demonstrate the great efficiency of all good screenwriting. For example, a sequence that proves important later, when Matty's niece catches her giving oral sex to Ned, lasts no more than ten seconds. Visual storytelling also is very strong here, letting pictures alone tell the story whenever possible.

E.T.
written by Melissa Mathison

E.T. is an excellent movie to study for its rising conflict with increased jeopardy to the protagonist, for its magical moments, for its gentle humor and for its integration of subplot and main plot.

STRUCTURAL ANALYSIS
Note: times refer to edited TV version

Hook (1 min.) We begin with a bang, a flying saucer in a forest, its alien creatures collecting plant samples.

Complication (3-5 min.) Then a truckload of humans arrives, and the aliens race to escape. But one gets stranded. This is E.T.

Call to Action (13 min.) Our protagonist, a boy named Elliot, hears a noise outside (8 min.), and when he goes to investigate, something returns a ball he throws (9 min.). But his older brother and his friends don't believe him that something is out there. Investigating again, the boy finds E.T.—and, what is essential, tries to befriend him, despite his strange looks.

Act One Plot Point (25-30 min.) Elliot brings E.T. into his bedroom, keeping him as a kind of playmate and pet, beginning a relationship with the alien. Finally he shows E.T. to his brother and sister, a secret between them all.

Midpoint Plot Point (53 min.) E.T. manages to communicate that he is from outer space—and that he wants to go home. Despite Elliot's wanting him to stay, the kids help E.T. concoct a machine that can call his people to fetch him (60 min.).

Act Two Plot Point (73 min.) But human investigators have traced E.T., and here—with E.T. very sick—is where they find and capture him. All seems lost, with E.T. getting sicker by the moment and being treated like a frog in a lab class.

Resolution (90-107 min.) But when Elliot says to E.T., on what is presumably the alien's deathbed, "I love you," this proves to be a power that revives E.T. (the boy's and the alien's feelings are connected). Later (94 min.) Elliot, with his brother's help, steals the truck in which E.T. is held—and the chase begins to get to the forest where E.T.'s people are coming to pick him up. E.T. goes home.

NOTES

E.T. weaves plot and subplot into a narrative of rising tension and increased danger to "the good guys." Throughout the film, to the end of Act Two, the "humans" after E.T. are shown progressively on the trail and getting closer, in short visual scenes. For example, at 23, 34, 54, 65 and 71 minutes we are reminded that E.T. is being pursued—and then, of course, the humans arrive to study him and take him away. This reminder of danger, and our knowledge that the humans are getting closer and closer, increases jeopardy to the plan to get E.T. home.

Visual storytelling is also very strong here. Both the sequence in the forest that is the story's hook and the chase at the end that leads to its climax are virtually without dialogue. Here a picture is worth a thousand words—and it is instructive to see how these "silent actions" are treated rhetorically in the screenplay.

E.T. also is filled with moments of gentle humor, most of it a result of this alien's total charm (unlike all the monsters that came before and after).

But at root, this is a very human story, about a lonely boy who finally gets his playmate—and then must learn to say goodbye (after saving E.T. with the power of love). The original title of this script was *A Boy's Life*, which gets to the heart of the story, though admittedly very less a commercial title.

E.T. is well worth studying over and over again.

My Dinner With Andre
written by Wallace Shawn and Andre Gregory

Those who fight the 3-act paradigm as a formula that takes the soul out of film storytelling often point to movies like My Dinner With Andre *as an example of a movie that breaks the rules. Indeed, this film does take many liberties with how movies are usually made in the U.S. This, after all, is a movie almost totally shot while two men have dinner together. However, one rule that is not broken here is the rule of beginning-middle-end storytelling! By its use of the 3-act paradigm,* My Dinner With Andre *demonstrates the power and flexibility of the paradigm, not its bankruptcy.*

STRUCTURAL ANALYSIS

Hook (1 min.) Comic character hook about the busy life of a playwright, going to the stationery store, the Xerox machine, doing the "errands of your trade."

Complication (2-3 min.) Wally, the playwright, is having dinner with Andre, a man he's been avoiding for years.

Call to Action (8 min.) Wally prods Andre to tell him what he's been up to (asking questions relaxes him).

Act One Plot Point (21, 35 min.) Wally gets more and more hooked by, and interested in, Andre's story of working with Grotowski in Poland.

Midpoint Plot Point (53 min.) Wally becomes an active participant in the conversation, sharing a bad theater experience. Later he takes issue with some of Andre's remarks (64 min.) (he likes his electric blanket).

Act Two Plot Point (76-7 min.) Wally is strongly on the defensive—is it still legitimate for writers even to write? Andre has a conspiracy theory about the present being a new Dark Ages, in which consumers build their own prison (79 min.).

Climax and Resolution Wally and Andre represent two different worldviews, the former the rational man, the latter the mystic. There is no final consensus.

NOTES

My Dinner With Andre is driven by the inherent interest in Andre's unusual and mystical experiences, punctuated increasingly by Wally's comic common sense. The art of conversation is far from dead here. More importantly, the talk twists and turns within the time-proven structure of beginning-middle-end storytelling.

1990s movies

Thelma & Louise
written by Callie Khouri

Thelma & Louise is a wonderful movie to study for the use of "buddies" as protagonists. In a buddy picture, two strong leads share the central focus, each with their own character arc, sometimes in conflict with one another. In some buddy pictures, one character clearly is the lead; in others, as here, both are equally strong roles, and the movie is propelled by the drama of this joint-protagonist.

STRUCTURAL ANALYSIS

Hook (1-7 min.) Thelma & Louise are planning a vacation together but from the start we learn that Thelma hasn't told her husband, who clearly won't approve. Will she get permission to go? Or will she go without telling him? She ends up doing the latter, leaving him a note.

Complication (9 min.) Thelma convinces Louise to make a quick stop at a bar, rather than continuing quickly to the secluded cabin that is their destination. Here is where the trouble will begin. They start drinking, celebrating.

Call to Action (18 min.) When a guy takes Thelma into the parking lot for fresh air, he makes an aggressive move on her—and, in fact, would have raped her if Louise had not intervened with a gun (that Thelma brought for protection). The women are moving off when the guy makes a lewd remark. Spontaneously, Louise turns and shoots him. Now everything has really changed: they enter a new world, the "extraordinary" world of being criminals on the run.

Act One Plot Point (33 min.) What should they do? Thelma wants to go to the police. Louise says no one would believe it was self-defense. Now we see the antagonist: the sexist culture in which they live, that leads them to decide there is no justice for them through lawful channels. Louise decides she is making a run for Mexico. Thelma will come to the decision to join her.

Midpoint Plot Point (66 min.) They need money for the escape, and Louise's boyfriend delivers an amount equal to her savings, $6700. But Thelma has taken a liking to a hitchhiking cowboy, ending up in a motel room with him (where she gets "fucked right" for the first time). The cowboy skips with the money. Now the women are broke. How will they get to Mexico? Thelma will rob a market, using the technique her cowboy one-night stand shared with her.

Act Two Plot Point (105 min.) Their trouble has escalated: from accidental shooting to robbing a store; and then to locking a policeman who stops them in the trunk of his squad car. Now a warrant is out for their arrest for murder, "dead or alive." They are considered armed and desperate. Moreover, through the cowboy (with whom the ever-trusting Thelma was honest), the police know they are making a run to Mexico.

Climax and Resolution (120-5 min.) The women are surrounded by police and trapped at the Grand Canyon. They decide to drive off the edge rather than to face the consequences in a sexist society where they will receive no justice, a suicide that becomes their final act of newfound power.

NOTES

This movie offers many tips for beginning writers:

Visual storytelling: from the beginning, we learn that Thelma and Louise are different kinds of people by seeing how they pack for the vacation. Without dialogue, we learn that Louise is neat and proper, Thelma spontaneous and wild.

Foreshadowing: Louise refuses to go through Texas on the way to Mexico (from Oklahoma), making their trip much longer than necessary. There's a reason for this, as we'll learn later: Texas is where she herself was raped.

Scene economy: This script has excellent scene design, which is to say scenes are not longer than they have to be. For example, when the police reach Louise's boyfriend, two lines of dialogue suffice: are you so and so? Arkansas State Police. Cut. A beginner would extend this scene to half a page, a page, even more, with useless time-consuming questions that do nothing but slow down the narrative drive.

Rising jeopardy: Film stories need to have rising action, a movement in which jeopardy to the protagonist increases. This is beautifully handled here, with Thelma and Louise getting deeper and deeper into trouble with each new twist and turn in the action.

Comic moments: This movie is also filled with great comic moments. For example, when they take the policeman hostage, Thelma tells Louise to shoot the radio. She does. "The police radio, Louise," says Thelma.

Changing roles: In the beginning of this double-protagonist story, Louise is the stronger one and calls the shots. But after Thelma loses their escape money, she robs a store and gains new strength herself, later instigating the escape from the policeman, finally being able to say, "I think I have a knack for this." Neither character is stagnant, each grows, but in different ways: the meek if crazy Thelma finding new strength, the more "controlled" Louise finding new intimacy and sharing with Thelma.

Shakespeare in Love
written by Marc Norman and Tom Stoppard

Shakespeare in Love, darling of the 1998 Oscars, is a Hollywood movie at its best: full of romance, big themes, and great wit. Naturally it follows 3-act structure very closely.

STRUCTURAL ANALYSIS

<u>Hook</u> (0 min.) A debtor is being tortured. He promises to pay off his debt with revenue from a new comedy by Shakespeare, *Romeo and Ethel, the Pirate's Daughter.*

<u>Complication</u> (3 min.) But Shakespeare has a writing block and is getting nothing done.

<u>Call to Action</u> (27-9 min.) After a "false" call to action, when Shakespeare takes Rosaline to be his muse (until he catches her in bed with someone else), Will meets Viola at a dance and falls for her. As a result of meeting her, he starts writing like crazy, even writing her a sonnet.

<u>Act One Plot Point</u> (35 min.) Rehearsals for Will's new play begin. A young actor, Thomas (who is Viola in disguise), impresses Will.

<u>Midpoint Plot Point</u> (44-8 min.) Will learns Thomas is Viola. They kiss, make love. "It's a new world," says Viola. But she must marry Wessex (37 min.).

<u>Act Two Plot Point</u> (83 min.) The theater is closed down and Thomas is revealed to be a woman, Viola. (See Notes).

<u>Climax and Resolution</u> (87-113 min.) A new stage is offered for Will's play, *Romeo and Juliet*, now a tragic tale about star-crossed lovers (i.e., Will and Viola). The man playing Juliet can't perform and, arriving after her marriage, Viola is a last-minute substitute. The play is a hit. The Queen, who knows all, lets a lady on stage pass. Will and Viola say their goodbyes, she leaves to Virginia with her husband, and Will begins *Twelfth Night*, naming a character Viola, his heroine for all time.

NOTES

Shakespeare in Love uses a number of devices we find in the Bard's plays, such as disguises and mistaken identity. Marlowe's popularity and rivalry are used to great comic effect, then turned temporarily tragic when Marlowe is murdered and Will feels responsible. No doubt Stoppard was brought in to give this story much of the high wit that embellishes an already good story.

Structurally there are several things especially interesting about this script. As noted above, there is a "false" call to action before the one that moves into the focus of the story. There also are competing "low points" for the end of Act Two: the revelation that Will is married, the death of Marlowe, the wedding of Viola. How do we know which is the "real" end of Act Two? I believe it's the closing of the play where Viola is revealed to be a woman because the play (not weddings or murders) provides the context for the resolution of the story. That is, reopening the play (not Will's getting a divorce or Viola's avoiding marriage) is the context of the resolution, the stage upon which the lovers can express their love in its most poetic expression. The structure of the play thus has focus in its three acts: Act One, pre-play to the beginning of rehearsal; Act Two, the rehearsal and closing; Act Three, reopening and performance. The play provides the stage and context for the love affair.

The Sixth Sense
written by M. Night Shyamalan

The Sixth Sense is a thriller about a child psychiatrist trying to redeem a failed episode in his past by helping a disturbed boy. The movie packs a great surprise ending and a brilliant piece of acting in the role of the boy.

STRUCTURAL ANALYSIS

Hook (0-1 min.) A woman fetching wine from the basement thinks she hears something. Something creepy is going on.

Complication (4-5 min.) A former patient of Dr. Malcolm Crowe has broken into the house. He shoots the doctor, then kills himself, as the wife watches in horror.

Call to Action (9 min.) The following fall, Crowe takes on another case, to help a disturbed boy.

Act One Plot Point (24-6, 34 min.) Crowe commits himself to the case, even being late for his anniversary dinner. He sees this as a second chance, a chance to redeem himself, and he doesn't want it to slip away. But the wife finds him distant, and this case is hurting his marriage. Later, at school, the boy becomes verbally violent and shows he is able to see people's secrets. He has some kind of power.

Midpoint Plot Point (47 min.) The boy shares his secret with Crowe: he can see dead people.

Act Two Plot Point (65-6, 69 min.) Crowe says he is going to quit the case. He admits failure. He wants his marriage back like it was. But he hasn't really believed the boy, who says "how can you help me if you don't believe me?" Then Crowe hears strange voices on an interview tape—could they be ghosts, the voices of dead people?

Climax and Resolution (81-9, 94-6 min.) Crowe gives the boy tools to help himself: the ghosts appear because they want help. So help them. He is able to help a grieving father and even his own mother with their experiences of death. In a surprise ending, when Crowe returns home to work on his marriage, we learn that he actually was killed, not wounded, when he was shot at the beginning of the movie. His final death was delayed so he could redeem himself first and now he tells his sleeping wife, "I think I can go now."

NOTES
The Sixth Sense is full of suspense and surprises. It's a gripping movie.

Independence Day
written by Dean Devlin and Roland Emmerich

Independence Day *is the kind of movie Hollywood does well, a fast-moving action tale with superb special effects. Although it has some weakness in protagonist focus, it is well worth studying for its excellent scene design and economy.*

STRUCTURAL ANALYSIS
Hook (1 min.) A strange shadow crosses the lunar landscape, as an object heads for Earth.
Complication (2-3 min.) On Earth, radio signals from the object are picked up. There's something from another world out there—and it's slowing down.
Call to Action (16 min.) The President refuses to join the evacuation of government in D.C. He's staying with the ship to see what this object is.
Act One Plot Point (26-7 min.) "We're not alone," the President tells the nation—and panic and chaos result. David, a techie, knows the aliens are poised to attack.
Midpoint Plot Point (45-9 min.) The aliens attack, destroying major cities. Air Force One barely escapes.
Act Two Plot Point (89 min.) The end of the world appears at hand. The U.S.'s best nuclear device fails to penetrate the protective shield of the attacking space ship.
Climax and Resolution (97, 120-30 min.) David gets the idea of giving the spaceship a virus, destroying its protective shield. The President himself flies a jet and it is his strike that first damages the spaceship. The Earth is saved.

NOTES

Independence Day has a tight scene structure—scenes are short and focused, each driving the story forward. Moments of high action are followed by more reflective quiet scenes, a typical pattern in story pacing. The stakes, especially on the ride through the last act, are always getting raised—the situation looks worse than it did, or a seeming victory is quickly followed by a reversal and greater challenge. For example, just when it appears the "earthlings" can "fire at will," they run out of missiles—until an alcoholic crop duster pilot shows up late, with all his missiles ready to go.

There are four important character arcs in this story, and the failure of the President or anyone else to become the clear protagonist is the weakness here, although it is not a crippling one in a story so packed with action and special effects.

2000s movies

A Beautiful Mind
written by Akiva Goldsman

A Beautiful Mind is told in such a way that we are reminded that dramatic structure is about the order of events presented to the audience—because we learn that much of the first half of the story is an hallucination! Clear and strong structure nonetheless.

STRUCTURAL ANALYSIS

<u>Hook</u> Young math grad students at Princeton are challenged to use their brains in the fight against the Soviet Union in the early Cold War.

<u>Complication</u> John Nash is a social misfit obsessed with finding an original idea for his thesis.

<u>Call to Action</u> He gets his original idea, to prove Adam Smith wrong, and writes a brilliant, original thesis.

<u>Act One Plot Point</u> His genius gets him secret work as a code breaker for the Department of Defense.

<u>Midpoint Plot Point</u> As the secret work becomes more dangerous than he anticipated, Nash gets more paranoid and erratic in behavior until he finally is institutionalized. There we learn that the story above is his hallucination—there is no spy work for the Defense Department! The characters we've seen are figments of his imagination.

Act Two Plot Point Back home, he stops taking meds and the hallucinations escalate until his wife is about to leave him and he is about to be re-institutionalized as soon as she signs the papers.

Climax and Resolution Nash convinces his wife not to sign so he can "cure himself" and he learns to live with his hallucinations. He goes on to win the Nobel Prize.

NOTES

A Beautiful Mind shocks us with its midpoint twist because we experience the hallucinations as real, just as Nash does. A nice touch.

Monster's Ball
written by Milo Addica & Will Rokos

Monster's Ball *portrays a love affair between two troubled souls, one a corrections officer with a racist upbringing, the other the black widow of a man he executed.*

STRUCTURAL ANALYSIS

Hook The first thing a man does upon waking in the morning is throw up. What's going on?

Complication The man is our protagonist, a corrections officer. So was his father, a racist, and so is his son, who has black friends. After an altercation, the son commits suicide in front of his father.

Call to Action The man quits his job at the prison. He can't take it any longer. First by chance, and then by choice, he becomes acquainted with and helps the black widow of a man he executed.

Act One Plot Point He and the widow begin a love affair.

Midpoint Plot Point When the widow meets his racist father, she breaks up with him. He puts his father in a rest home. When the widow is evicted from her home, he takes her in. They begin living together.

Act Two Plot Point The woman discovers a portrait by her late husband of her lover, the former prison guard. She puts two and two together. It looks like it's over.

Climax and Resolution But she says nothing. He comes home with ice cream. "I think we're going to make it," he says. They need each other.

NOTES

Monster's Ball is one of the best movies you can study for subtext: strong visual storytelling and everything happening below the surface of the very spare dialogue. Deep emotions are communicated here, helped considerably by the very strong performances of the two major characters. What this story is about, the need of two people with similar emotional issues for one another, is never stated explicitly. This is a wonderful story driven by subtext.

My Big Fat Greek Wedding
written by Nia Vardalos

My Big Fat Greek Wedding is an entertaining light comedy with few surprises but lots of charm and a big heart.

STRUCTURAL ANALYSIS

<u>Hook</u> A Greek father to his 30-year-old unmarried daughter: you are getting old and need to marry a good Greek boy.

<u>Complication</u> Since childhood the daughter has rebelled against her family and Greek background.

<u>Call to Action</u> She betters herself by going to computer school and taking over the extended family's travel agency.

<u>Act One Plot Point</u> She meets a guy and starts dating.

<u>Midpoint Plot Point</u> He asks her to marry him—and although he's not Greek, she says yes.

<u>Act Two Plot Point</u> The father thinks the marriage can never work—their roots are too different.

<u>Climax and Resolution</u> The father notes that although they are apples and oranges, at least they are both fruit. It can work. He buys them a house as a wedding present—right next door to his.

NOTES

The low point is really not very low but it hardly matters amidst all the fun.

O Brother, Where Art Thou?
written by Ethan and Joel Coen

Homer's Odyssey is moved to the Depression South in this whimsical and musical stylized comedy. The traditional 3-act paradigm is stretched here to fit within the "hero's journey" structure of Homer, but all the structural foundations remain.

STRUCTURAL ANALYSIS

<u>Hook</u> (1 min.) 3 convicts escape the chain gang—Everett, Pete and Delmar.

<u>Complication</u> (6 min.) Chased by the authorities and their dogs, the threesome meet a blind old man on the railroad tracks who casts their future as a great journey with surprising results.

<u>Call to Action</u> (22 min.) A black guitar player leads them to an out-of-the-way radio station where they pose as an old-timey singing group, the Soggy Bottom Boys, and "sing into a can" for money. The song (23 min.) is a spectacular version of Man of Constant Sorrow.

<u>Act One Plot Point</u> (37 min.) Their song is a statewide hit, and the radio station folks want to find them to sign them to a contract. So now they are twice pursued: as escaped convicts (ordinary world) and as musical stars (extraordinary world).

<u>Midpoint Plot Point</u> (58-60, 66-70 min.) There are two major midpoint twists. In the first, Everett is revealed to have a wife and large family, all daughters. But his wife, who divorced him when he was in prison, is set to remarry. Everett later confesses that there's no buried treasure, to which he was supposed to be leading his fellow escapees.

<u>Act Two Plot Point</u> (93 min.) The threesome is finally captured by the authorities. Their graves are dug, the ropes to hang them are ready. Everett prays for the first time in his life.

<u>Climax and Resolution</u> (95-101 min.) They are rescued by a flash flood: a TVA project is flooding the valley. Everett gets his wife back, though they are still bickering.

NOTES

O Brother, Where Art Thou? has a long, meandering first act that does not get boring because it is filled with Homeric encounters with eccentric characters along the journey. There also is a "false low point" (75) when a political candidate blows their cover as the Soggy Bottom Boys, but the crowd genuinely loves their music and boos the politician off. This is the moment when Everett's wife returns to him, satisfied that he is somebody after all. Much of the charm of this movie is in its music and stylized use of it—even a Klan meeting is given visual and musical beauty by its choreography. This movie is another unusual and original accomplishment by the Coen brothers.

Traffic
written by Stephen Gaghan

Traffic *is an intense and gripping drama about the drug trade, told in three interweaving and related story lines. Powerful and real, the script/ movie is well designed with strong visual storytelling. Each story thread has its own dramatic structure.*

STRUCTURAL ANALYSIS

Hook (0-4 min.) Mexican state police bust some drug traffickers but the Mexican Army takes over the prisoners in custody. The Mexican cop and his partner define one of the three story lines.

Complication (10, 13 min.) In the second story line, two U.S. undercover agents are about to bust a dealer when local authorities screw it up. In the third, the daughter of a judge about to be appointed national drug czar is herself an addict. This drug czar is the main protagonist (hence played by the star, Michael Douglas).

Call to Action (16, 27 min.) The judge is appointed to be the drug czar. A Mexican Army general hires the cop to help him bust the Tijuana cartel.

Act One Plot Point (30 min.) The judge begins to put together his plan for the war on drugs; the U.S. undercover team makes a major arrest; and an arrest in the Mexican cartel is made. All the major story lines are now set up and moving forward.

Midpoint Plot Point (67, 76, 79 min.) The judge wants to think out of the box and come up with new ideas to fight drugs. Personally, he discovers that his daughter is addicted to hard drugs. A Mexican cop urges U.S. agents to take more interest in what is happening across the border.

Act Two Plot Point (107, 123, 127 min.) The partner of the Mexican cop is killed. The judge finds his daughter zonked and doing tricks in a drug house. The U.S. undercover agent, whose partner also is killed, finds his major witness poisoned before testifying.

Climax and Resolution (136, 138, 139 min.) The U.S. undercover agent manages to plant a bug in the house of the dealer who got off after the death of the witness. The judge and his wife attend treatment sessions with their daughter. The Mexican cop, who helped the U.S. make a bust, uses his payoff to have a ballpark built for kids.

NOTES

Traffic works so well because it tells its layered story so efficiently. The scenes are short and focused—in fact, the long 145-page script has 263 scenes! The short scenes, moving between the different story lines, keep the pacing strong and a sense of "what happens next?" holds our interest throughout.

Far From Heaven
written by Todd Haynes

Far From Heaven is a drama set in the 1950s about the perils of interracial friendship and flirting. Slow moving but excellent, with strong dramatic structure.

STRUCTURAL ANALYSIS

<u>Hook</u> The protagonist's husband is late for dinner. He's been arrested.

<u>Complication</u> The husband is gay. The family gardener died, replaced by his handsome black son.

<u>Call to Action</u> The wife convinces her husband to see a doctor to cure his "disease." She goes out of her way to befriend the black gardener.

<u>Act One Plot Point</u> She and the black gardener are seen in public together, starting vicious rumors about their relationship.

<u>Midpoint Plot Point</u> The husband announces his love for a man and wants a divorce. The wife fires the gardener.

<u>Act Two Plot Point</u> The gardener's daughter (he's a single parent) is attacked by school kids. The wife goes to see him and learns he is leaving town. No, she can't visit—interracial friendship between the sexes, and their mutual attraction, is too dangerous.

<u>Climax and Resolution</u> She rushes to the train station to see him off. And he still leaves. They cannot transcend their times.

NOTES

Ruthlessly honest, with a refusal to embrace the Hollywood ending. A fantastic film—but it sizzles beneath the surface, in its subtext, and is not for everyone.

Memento
written by Christopher Nolan

At first glance Memento *might seem to be without traditional dramatic structure, so different and circular are its storytelling strategies. However, this is not true. This "puzzle movie" stays true to the principles of traditional storytelling, which again attests to the power and flexibility of the paradigm.*

STRUCTURAL ANALYSIS

<u>Hook</u> (0 min.) A man asks himself, Where am I? He has a Polaroid of what appears to be a crime scene. He has scratches on his face.

<u>Complication</u> (7 min.) The man has no short-term memory.

<u>Call to Action</u> (15 min.) He is on a mission of revenge. He has a gun.

<u>Act One Plot Point</u> (22, 32 min.) He worries someone is setting him up, taking advantage of his condition, getting him to kill the wrong guy. We are in a world of repetition and paradox.

<u>Midpoint Plot Point</u> (67,73 min.) The woman who appears to have been helping him actually is using him. She even tells him so, knowing he won't remember.

<u>Act Two Plot Point</u> (104-6 min.) He finds and kills the man he believes raped and murdered his wife. But in reality he has killed Jimmy, a drug dealer, the woman above's boyfriend. A policeman (who for a time was the prime suspect for revenge) tells him the truth: he's been lying to himself to be happy because he can't face the truth.

<u>Climax and Resolution</u> (110 min.) The man sets up his own circular hell. He notes on the Polaroid of the cop not to trust him. He takes his murder victim's car and drug money. He sets up the conditions for an endless replaying of the same dilemma. He can't accept the truth.

NOTES

This is a gripping puzzle movie that uses a very unusual story strategy based on repetition and expansion, as fragments of the story reappear, grow, and reveal their relationships to one another. The journey of the audience through the paradigm mirrors the journey of the protagonist. In the end, it's been great fun but pretty much all head, no heart, and the movie doesn't linger long once the puzzle has been solved or dismissed.

About Schmidt
written by Alexander Payne & Jim Taylor

About Schmidt *is a drama and dark comedy about a man who feels his life is a waste but learns there is at least one thing he is doing right.*

STRUCTURAL ANALYSIS
Hook Schmidt is retiring from his insurance job.
Complication But he's not too happy about it. There's a big vacuum in his life.
Call to Action He tries to fill it by sponsoring a child in Africa.
Act One Plot Point His wife dies, leaving him alone. He hits the road in his RV.
Midpoint Plot Point He tries to convince his daughter to cancel her wedding to a guy not worthy of her.
Act Two Plot Point He decides he's failed at everything.
Climax and Resolution He gets his first letter from the African child and a drawing that shows him this, at least, is something he is doing right.

NOTES
Great performances help this dark comedy considerably. There are some Oscar roles here.

Adaptation
written by Charlie Kaufman & Donald Kaufman

Adaptation *is a witty sophisticated comedy about the difficulty of making a movie based on a book about orchids.*

STRUCTURAL ANALYSIS
Hook A screenwriter is filled with self-loathing.
Complication Pitching an adaptation of a book about orchids, he wants to avoid all Hollywood clichés and make a movie about real life.
Call to Action He gets the gig and starts on the adaptation.
Act One Plot Point He's having great difficulty, stuck in a world of false starts.
Midpoint Plot Point His twin brother, who just sold a Hollywood blockbuster, is invited in to help the protagonist finish his script. He is behind on deadlines.

<u>Act Two Plot Point</u> The twin believes the author of the book is having an affair with her main protagonist—they must follow her. But the protagonist is caught. "Let's kill him," the author says.

<u>Climax and Resolution</u> The screenwriter's life turns into a Hollywood movie, full of action and chases, and in the end his twin is killed. The screenwriter realizes how much he loved his brother, and this gives him the courage to tell a woman he loves her (she loves him back). He is looking on the bright side of life for the first time.

NOTES

Layers of fun and inside jokes about screenwriting make this story great fun for writers. But it also has a serious side, a story about trying to make a movie mirroring life turning into a life that mirrors movies, a kind of philosophical joke. This film is more complex than a single viewing reveals.

The Hours
written by David Hare

A brilliant adaptation of the award-winning novel. The story of Virginia Woolf's struggle to write *Mrs. Dalloway* and with her own sanity is reflected in the lives of two women a generation apart, in the 1950s and today, whose lives finally cross.

STRUCTURAL ANALYSIS

<u>Hook</u> Virginia writes her suicide note and walks into the river.

<u>Complication</u> 20 years earlier, she is struggling to begin a book and not eating, not being a "good patient" for her husband.

<u>Call to Action</u> She decides what her book is about: a woman's life in a single day. This gets reflected in the lives of the two women a generation apart.

<u>Act One Plot Point</u> Virginia is cooking, her muse active. Mrs. Dalloway must die.

<u>Midpoint Plot Point</u> Virginia rebels against her caregivers, including her husband. Her sanity is her own business. Mrs. Dalloway will not die. The 1950s woman can't go through with her suicide.

<u>Act Two Plot Point</u> A poet with AIDS dies (the son of the 1950s woman, the soul mate of the present day lesbian). Virginia decides it is the poet who must die, the visionary – herself.

<u>Climax and Resolution</u> The two women choose life. Virginia (the poet must die) walks into the river.

NOTES

This is one story, the story of an emotional journey through life by three women of three different generations, all asking the same questions about their lives and their deaths. From this perspective, the dramatic structure is seen to be tight and traditional (beginning-middle-end storytelling), great testimony to the power of 3-act structure.

APPENDIX 2

The 3-Act Paradigm Work Sheet
by Charles Deemer

TITLE:

AUTHOR:

LOGLINE:

(Note: page references below are guidelines and can vary.)

ACT ONE

The Hook [first scene if possible; no later than several pages in] (we have to know what happens next):

The Complication [scene after the hook if possible; certainly before page 10] (the hero's initial predicament):

The Hero's Call to Action [about 12-20 pages in] (s/he's going for the "goal"):

First Act Plot Point [about 25-30 pages in] (a startling turn of events):

ACT TWO

Hero's Goal (what s/he wants now):

Midpoint Plot Point [about 50-60 pages in] (another turn of events, possible new goal):

Act Two Plot Point [about 75-90 pages in] (major reversal, all appears lost):

ACT THREE

Hero's Goal (what is the showdown about?):

Climax & Resolution [100-120 pages in] (how does the hero win?):

APPENDIX 3

Screenwriting Contests

The best and safest way to test your screenwriting wings is to enter screenwriting competitions. *Any* contest can make you feel good if you win, as well as give evidence, validation, that you are doing something right.

The best resource for locating contests is online at:

> *http://www.moviebytes.com/directory.cfm*

Every serious beginning screenwriter should enter the following two contests every year.

1. Nicholl Screenwriting Fellowship

> Academy Foundation
> 8949 Wilshire Blvd.
> Beverly Hills, CA 90211-1972
> 310-247-3000 (voice)

> Web: *http://www.oscars.org/academy/nichollindex.html*
> Contact: Greg Beal, Director
> Deadline: May 1
> Notification: mid-October
> Eligibility: Open to anyone.
> Entry Fee: $30
> Rules: No applicant may have earned more $1,000 for screenwriting. Scripts should be in standard form, 100-130 pages.
> Awards: Up to five $25,000 fellowships.

2. Austin Screenplay Competition

> Austin Heart of Film Festival Script & Film Competition
> 1600 Nuenueces
> Austin, TX 78701
> 800-310-3378 (voice)
> 512-478-6205 (fax)

> Contact: Barbara Morgan, Director
> Deadline: May 15
> Notification: October

Eligibility: Writers who have not earned money writing for television or film.

Entry Fee: $35

Rules: Submissions must include a two- or three-sentence synopsis. Screenplays will not be returned. Page should be 3-hole punched and bound by metal fasteners. Scripts in Adult and Family categories must be between 90 and 130 pages.

Awards: Two winners receive $3500 first place prizes, participation in the Heart of Film Mentorship Program, airfare and accommodations to attend the conference, and the HOF Bronze Award.

These are the two most important contests because they have solid track records. Even making the quarterfinals in either is prestigious and can result in requests for your script from producers and agents. If you are serious about screenwriting and not entering these two contests annually, you are missing the best potential quick start to a screenwriting career. Mike Rich (*Finding Forrester, The Rookie*) and Max Adams (*Excess Baggage*) are recent winners who started their screenwriting careers via Nicholl or Austin. The next one may be you.

You should check the Internet for the latest information on all contests. Fees do go up and personnel change.

APPENDIX 4

A Sample 10-week Syllabus

WEEK 1
From concept to logline to format

The contemporary screenplay is like a blueprint, and screenwriters are like architects. I prefer to call a screenwriter a *screenwright* to emphasize the importance of *craft* ("wright") in screenwriting.

A movie story often begins with a concept. Movie concepts are expressed as "**loglines**;" a logline is a pithy one- or several-sentence statement of your story. Often these involve what is called "**high concept**," an idea that can be quickly explained and easily understood. Also important is the story's **genre**, an important marketing device.

The vast majority of screenplays are **structured in three acts** (or some modification of three act structure). This is not as stifling to creativity or as limiting as some beginning writers think. Three-act structure is really a *cultural phenomenon*, not an aesthetic one, and speaks to the fact that in our culture audiences like to get their stories with a beginning, a middle and an end. Today "screenplay paradigms" have become a cottage industry, but all come out of Aristotle and three act (beginning/middle/end) structure.

Some beginning writers rebel against "structure" because they misinterpret structure as "formula," stifling creativity. Nothing could be farther from the truth. **You should think of structure *as grammar*,** as the relational rules that make film stories work.

Also important is *screenplay format*. If you take your screenwriting seriously, you are going to want to get software that does the grunt work of screenwriting automatically. Templates for word processing programs are the best bet if you can't afford screenplay software yet. **The important thing to remember about format is that it is rather precise and does not include anything that is the director's decision, such as camera angles**.

READING
Deemer, chapters 1-4

WRITING
Selected exercises.

WEEK 2
Screenplay structure

All screenplay stories have a beginning, middle and end. Focus is tight on the main character and his/her journey to overcome obstacles in order to reach a goal or satisfy a need. Screenplay structure gives dramatic movement to this journey in such a way that the stakes keep getting raised and tension increases. There are no wasted moments in a screenplay. **"American movies," wrote Richard Toscan, "are about what happens next."**

READING
Deemer, chapters 5-8.

WRITING
Select your project type (Act One or 30-min. script) and track (tree or forest) and turn them in (in writing). Everyone: Submit three loglines for original stories you might develop into a screenplay during this class. *A good logline is ONE sentence; two sentences max!* For example, "A lonely boy befriends a stranded alien and helps him escape from government scientists to catch a space ship home." *E.T.*, of course. Also: Selected exercises (optional).

WEEK 3
From the ordinary to the extraordinary: Understanding Act One

The burden of act one is this: to **introduce the hero**, called the protagonist, and the dramatic spine of the story, which usually is **a conflict between a goal of the hero and an obstacle** (represented by a villain or antagonist) standing in the way of reaching it.

The hook gets us immediately interested in what is happening. Usually **a complication** soon follows, moving the story toward the protagonist and his/her "dramatic problem" (what s/he wants, what is stopping success).

When we meet the hero, it usually is in "ordinary" circumstances, the hero's normal home turf. The "**call to action**" (to use mythic terminology) presents the hero with a goal, a desire, a puzzle, a challenge, that moves him/her into new and "extraordinary" turf.

This journey defines the story and makes up the focus of act one, so by the time we are 20-30 pages (20-30 minutes) into the story, we know who the hero is, what the hero wants, and what is in the way of getting it. If we learn all these things sooner, even better. Screenwriting is about writing with great economy.

READING
Deemer, chapter 9.

WRITING

Everyone: select the logline you will develop as your project. *Forest track only:* Write the hook for your script (no more than 5 pages for feature, 1-2 pages for 30 min.). Also: Selected exercises (optional).

WEEK 4
Increasing Jeopardy: Understanding Act Two

Most screenwriters say that writing act two is the hardest part of screenwriting. Act two is twice as long as acts one and two, for starters, and presents greater challenges than any other section of the screenplay.

Think of act two in two movements: the first half and the second half (this is why some people prefer to talk about a four-act structure, but this difference is merely semantic, don't lose any sleep over it). In the first half, we have a 25-30 page "module" that ends with **an important twist in the story, called "a plot point,"** that moves the narrative in a surprising new direction. The result of this usually is that the hero has a much harder task than it seemed at first. New and surprising challenges present themselves; things we thought we knew are "reversed," showing the opposite to be true.

This development through the first half of act two **raises the stakes for the hero**—and increases our interest and desire to know "what happens next." If you can keep your audience asking **"What happens next?,"** you are doing a good job, generally speaking. But in order to ask this question, we also have to care about the hero and want him/her to win in the end.

Act Two reaches the midpoint, then, by **spinning the story in a challenging new direction**.

READING

Deemer chapter 10.

WRITING

Tree track only: Submit a paradigm chart. Also write and submit the hook. Also: Selected exercises (optional).

WEEK 5
Creating Heroes for Stars: Keeping Focus in Act Two

Screenplays by beginning writers often make a mess of act two, and the problem commonly begins by losing focus on the hero. Subplots and minor characters, or the villain, take over the story.

One way to help prevent this from happening is to "cast yourself a superstar"—that is, imagine that a famous actor or actress is playing the role of your hero. This person is getting paid a fortune, and your producer wants him/her to earn every dime of it—by being in as many scenes as possible! If you remember to keep the spotlight on your hero, **putting the hero in as many scenes as possible**, you'll go far in making sure the focus of act two remains where it belongs, *on the hero and the hero's goal.*

So the last half of act two is even more challenging to write. Often the hero meets the new challenge with success and for a moment, about midway through this section of the story, it may appear that the hero is on the way to reaching the goal, meeting the challenge. But then an even greater and more difficult challenge presents itself, a surprising "plot point" that now points the hero toward defeat.

The challenge of act two, then, is one of structuring the narrative so that the hero is presented with greater challenges and is put in **increasing jeopardy**. The pace usually quickens in the last half of act two, moving toward the climax of the final act.

Take-home MIDTERM handed out this week.

READING
Deemer, chapter 11.

WRITING
Forest only: Complete the first draft of the first act of your feature or entire 30-minute screenplay. Also: Selected exercises (optional).

WEEK 6
Climax and Resolution: Understanding Act Three

In act three, the hero moves from the jaws of defeat to the mountain top of victory. We've all seen it a million times. It's really what movies are about.

This is much trickier to write than it may seem. We want the hero's victory to be genuine and earned, not some unconvincing ending slapped down by the writer. **The success of this final confrontation between hero and villain, protagonist and antagonist, depends largely on having a worthy "bad guy."** Writing villains is tricky because they have to be forceful, on the one hand, yet not so strong that they steal the focus and thunder away from the hero. We all know movies with villains we'll never forget.

The happy ending is standard in mainstream American movies, which in my view is unfortunate.

READING
Deemer, chapter 12.

WRITING

Tree only: Complete draft of act one of feature or entire 30-min. script. Also: Selected exercises (optional).

WEEK 7
Writing is Rewriting

I define a first draft as the process by which I understand what it is I want to write. As you write your screenplay, new things are going to occur to you along the way and you need to respond to them, one way or the other. **Writing is first and foremost *a process* - and the most essential part of that process is *rewriting*.**

Most students overwrite. They enter their scenes too early, taking time to set something up rather than beginning the scene in the heat of the action. They leave scenes too late, continuing to write after the scene has made its point. They overwrite action, using complex sentence structures and detailed description more appropriate to novel-writing than to the hugely concise and economical form of the screenplay. They write dialogue that makes all characters sound alike.

You can usually spot an overwritten screenplay without even reading it. Give it the "white space" test. A producer actually showed me this "test" —and it usually works. Flip the pages of a screenplay rapidly, looking for the amount of **white space** you see. If it's mostly "dark" language, pages coming by cluttered with words, then the screenplay very likely is overwritten.

A good screenplay is filled with white space! Action sections are short and separated by paragraphs (white space). Long dialogue is avoided (although Tarantino and others are bringing it back into fashion, which I'm glad to see). The script, as set down on paper, is "opened up" and given lots of room to breathe.

There is a reason for this. Most screenplays are not read—*they are skimmed*. They are skimmed because the person picking it up is facing a pile of hundreds of screenplays waiting to be looked at right after yours. If you clutter the page with language, requiring careful reading, you are shooting yourself in the foot. If you open up the script with white space, you are making it easier for the reader's eye to move over the material quickly—and this is your chance, in fact your only chance, to grab the attention of the reader.

Keep these "school of hard knocks"' lessons in mind when you rewrite.

READING
Deemer, chapters 13-14.

Turn in midterm.

WRITING
Everyone: Start rewriting your draft – nothing due this week but you can turn in rewritten pages if you like. Also: Selected exercises (optional).

WEEK 8
Marketing Your Script

The Internet has made marketing a lot easier for screenwriters because many independent production companies ("prodcos") are online and welcome email queries. This is the place to begin. You send an independent producer a query letter.

There is an art to writing a good query letter. A query letter is a *brief* letter in which you "pitch" your screenplay story and invite the recipient to request the script. **Never send off a screenplay without first sending a query letter and having the script requested**.

Where do you send your query letter? Begin with the online or print version of the *Hollywood Creative Directory*. Check out other online and print resources. If the producer has an email address, query electronically; otherwise, send a letter ("snail mail").

What about getting an agent? Many beginning writers worry about this hurdle much too soon. The fact is, many independent prodcos will read your script as long as you fill out their release form. You'll have a better shot at getting an agent—and studios and major resources will require that you have an agent—after you have prodco interest and several scripts under your belt.

READING
Deemer, chapter 15.

WRITING
Everyone: Finish rewriting the draft of your script and submit the second draft.
Also: Selected exercises (optional).

WEEK 9
Building a Screenwriting Career

Building a screenwriting career means different things to different people. I am a playwright who also writes screenplays and that distinction is important to me. This self-concept defines my approach to screenwriting.

So the first thing you have to do is **decide how screenwriting fits into your life**. Is it your passion, the only thing you want to do? Is it a stepping block on the way to becoming a filmmaker? Is it something you are looking into? Do you think it's a way to get rich? Why are you writing screenplays?

Choose your movie concepts carefully. Studios will purchase poorly written screenplays. Why? *For the concept*. They can always hire a seasoned writer to "fix" it.

Good movie story concepts are much harder to come up with than you think, and as you gain more experience you will find that you are spending much more time thinking up your concept and discarding ideas that you would have rushed into script earlier on.

Develop a marketing plan. Most writers would rather write than market their work. But marketing is essential and even when you have an agent, the burden of marketing belongs to the writer. I devote one day a week to marketing and strongly urge you to create your own "plan" once you are ready to enter the marketplace.

But don't rush into the marketplace too early. Again, you can shoot yourself in the foot by doing so. Test the waters first by entering some screenplay contests and querying some small prodcos.

Should you move to LA? There are definite advantages to living in LA if you are a screenwriter. You are where the action is, and you are available for "meetings" at the drop of a hat. If screenwriting is your one and only passion, then I strongly urge you to look into moving there.

However, many writers sell spec scripts who do *not* live in LA. Others write screenplays as part of a larger career—for example, I am primarily a playwright and teacher who also writes screenplays and although I grew up in LA, you couldn't pay me enough to move back on a permanent basis.

But if screenwriting is your one passion, and you want to work through the studio system rather than with indies (many of whom are located out of LA), then you'd better look seriously at a move.

Expect a lot of rejection in the screenwriting business. You need to continue despite rejection.

READING
Deemer, chapter 16.

WRITING
Submit a query letter to an independent producer in which you "pitch" your screenplay.

Nothing due. Use this time to prepare final draft and class presentation for next week. Also: Selected exercises (optional).
Take-home portion of final (if any) passed out.

WEEK 10
Review and wrap-up

Review and/or presentation of class projects and/or in-class final exam.

READING
None.

WRITING
Final projects due. Ideally, this should be a third draft.

Take-home final due (if any) or in-class final during finals week.